......the illustrated guide to......

brewing
beer

the illustrated guide to
brewing
beer

A COMPREHENSIVE HANDBOOK OF BEGINNING HOMEBREWING

Matthew Schaefer

Skyhorse Publishing

Skyhorse Publishing books may be purchased in bulk at special discounts for sales promotion, corporate gifts, fund-raising, or educational purposes. Special editions can also be created to specifications. For details, contact the Special Sales Department. Skyhorse Publishing, 307 West 36th Street, 11th Floor, New York, NY 10018 or info@skyhorsepublishing.com.

Skyhorse® and Skyhorse Publishing® are registered trademarks of Skyhorse Publishing, Inc.®, a Delaware corporation.

www.skyhorsepublishing.com

10 9 8 7 6 5 4 3 2 1

Library of Congress Cataloging-in-Publication Data

Schaefer, Matthew.
  The illustrated guide to brewing beer : a comprehensive handbook of beginning homebrewing / Matthew Schaefer.
      p. cm.
  Includes bibliographical references and index.
  ISBN 978-1-61608-463-9 (pbk. : alk. paper)
1. Beer. 2. Brewing. I. Title.
  TP577.S33 2011
  641.87'3—dc23

                                    2011030377

Printed in China

For my son, Evan,
and for my wife, Kimberly,
who allowed me to write this while she rocked Evan to sleep

CONTENTS

INTRODUCTION

WHY BREW? There are probably as many answers as there are brewers out there, and one would presume that before picking up this book that you have come to some semblance of an answer yourself. For me, the beauty of brewing is in the craft—the chance to start with raw ingredients and carefully shape them into a beverage that I can enjoy and share with others. The ability to control the nuances of flavor, body, and aroma, to bring the end product as close to my idea of the ideal, is what keeps me coming back batch after batch.

I have some recipes that I have been working on for fifteen years. With each batch, I take detailed notes about my process and the end result: Carefully noting the color, flavor, body, mouthfeel, head retention, and aroma. Slowly tweaking the recipe with each successive batch. Diligently trying to reach a fleeting concept of what I think the perfect porter, IPA, or English bitter should be.

And the art of homebrewing gives the modern homebrewer a never-ending palette of ingredients and processes to choose from. Homebrew shops are once again experiencing a resurgence, and the availability of high-quality ingredients over the Internet has made finding even once-obscure grains, hops, and yeast strains easier than at any other time in history.

A good homebrew store, such as Brooklyn Homebrew, has a large selection of grains and equipment.

While the craft of brewing can become maddeningly complex, it by no means has to be. It can be said that grain almost wants to become beer. Given the basic conditions, beer almost makes itself. Leave bread or grain soaking in water long enough and you may very well end up with a basic beer, although it will probably not be particularly good. With a little bit of effort and knowledge, though, the homebrewer can make quite good beer and, with a little bit of practice, truly great beer can be made in your home with readily available ingredients and fairly simple equipment. While this book can't give you the experience that will come with practice, it strives to give you the knowledge that you will need to get there.

The process of homebrewing is fairly straightforward. It is the job of the homebrewer to give yeast access to sugars in a clean and sanitized environment. The all-grain brewer starts by soaking malted barley in hot water in order to cause a reaction that converts the complex carbohydrate starches in the barley to simple sugars. This process is called "mashing." The extract brewer skips the "mash," and uses commercially prepared malt extract added to water as a source of sugar. Both processes leave the brewer with a sweet liquid called "wort." The wort is boiled and then rapidly cooled. Yeast is introduced to the cooled wort and allowed to do its job, which is to break down the sugars and, ultimately, produce alcohol.

From this simple explanation, you can readily see that two of the most important aspects of the brewing process are the underlying ingredients (malted barley or malt extract) and yeast. And controlling these two factors goes a long way toward making great beer. The next two important factors are cleanliness and temperature control, but we will get further into that in the chapters to come.

········· the illustrated guide to ·······

brewing
beer

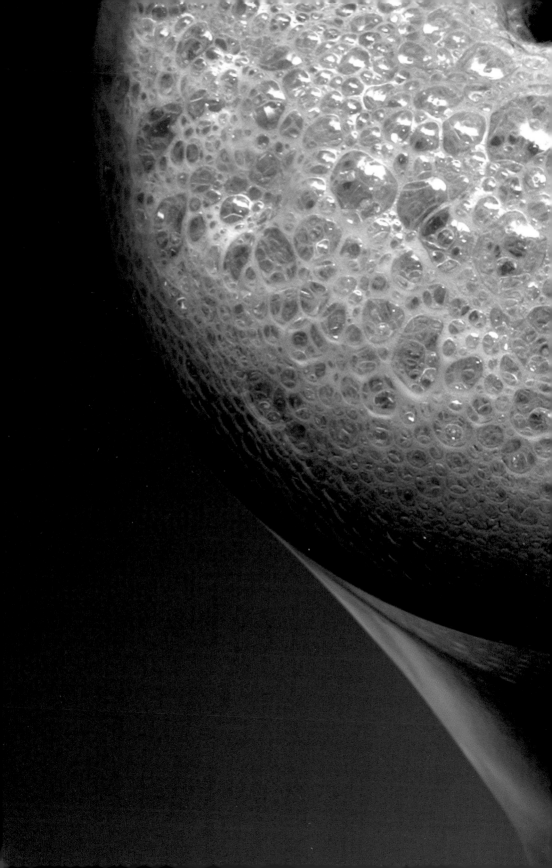

PART I

Brewing

IN MOST ACTIVITIES, fundamentals come first, and it is the same with brewing. Brewing is not unlike cooking where a recipe is meaningless unless you know what to do with the ingredients. The following chapters introduce you to the basic procedures that will take you from "grain to glass." They are by no means comprehensive, but they will guide you on very first steps that you will need to take on your path to brewing your own beer.

At times, these instructions may seem complicated, but I assure you that everything that you need to do is quite simple. Take it slow, use common sense, and stay calm. Remember, people have been brewing beer successfully for thousands of years despite knowing less about brewing than you will when you finish even the first few chapters.

WHETHER YOU ARE an extract brewer or all-grain brewer, an understanding of the process from grain to glass will help you understand the procedure that you will follow to make your own beer. A basic set of instructions will give you a list of not only the ingredients that you are going to use and what you need to do but also will present you with prohibitions and warnings that can become confusing if not downright intimidating. But with a little bit of knowledge, you can make sense of these instructions and enjoy the process.

1
THE BREWING PROCESS: AN OVERVIEW

Beer starts with barley, and in most instances, the barley is malted and kilned before it ever gets to the brewer. In the malting process barley is soaked in water until it starts to germinate. Germination is the process wherein the plant sprouts from the seed, and barley is nothing more than the seed of the barley plant. If you were growing barley this sprouted seed would become your new plant. But when you are creating malted barley this process is halted and the grain is dried out. The germination and malting is a very important

PHOTO COURTESY OF GOODBREWING.COM

part of the process as it makes various enzymes available that are necessary during the mash. Barley is primarily starch, and in the right environment the enzymes present in the malted barley will break down the starch into the sugars needed by the yeast to make alcohol.

Once the barley has been malted, it will be kilned by circulating hot air through the grains. Much of the flavor and color characteristics of the barley are developed during this process. The longer the kilning, and the hotter the kiln, the darker the malt will become. There are countless types of malts with colors ranging from straw to black, and each provides not only a color component, but a flavor component as well. Later during the brewing process, the brewer will select a "grain bill" of various malts and other non-malted grains, which will influence flavor, color, mouthfeel, and head retention.

Before the brewer can use the malt, the malt must be crushed. Most homebrew stores and Internet retailers will offer the homebrewer the option of buying grain either whole or pre-crushed. Whether you crush the grains yourself or not, the goal is to break up the grain kernel so that the starches are available during the mashing process—the finer the crush, the more starch that is available. The caveat is that you don't want to crush the grain too fine, or it will be difficult to separate the liquid from the spent grain at the end of the mashing process. At the end of the mash the grain husks will form a filter bed, allowing you to filter out the crushed grain from the wort.

To conduct the mash, the brewer mixes the crushed grain with hot water, and then allows the mash to sit at a temperature (usually) between 148 and 158 degrees Fahrenheit. The specific temperature of the water will favor certain enzymes over others. During this time the enzymes that were made available during the malting process work to break down the starches and convert them to sugars. The mash is complete once there is no starch left to convert. This usually takes between an hour and an hour and a half.

When the mash is done, the next step is to separate the liquid from the grain. This is called "lautering." The liquid, which has now become wort, is slowly drained from the mash, usually from a spigot at the bottom of the mash vessel. As mentioned, the grain will set-

PHOTO COURTESY OF PHIL SHAW

ABOVE: A sample of grains taken from a mash.

tle and form a filter bed that will filter the wort. The first wort to be drawn from the vessel is cloudy with bits of grain and husk. This is returned to the mash, until the filter bed is fully established and the wort runs clear.

The next step of the process can be handled in one of two ways, which will be discussed later on, but the basic idea is that the grains need to be rinsed. The wort is very sweet and sticky, and it will cling to the grains. The grains must be washed to collect all of the residual sugars. This is called "sparging." One way to accomplish this is to completely drain the wort from the mash and then mix in a measured amount of hot water. The sugars will dissolve into the hot water, which can then be drained and added to the wort. This is called "batch sparging." This is opposed to "fly sparging," which attempts to drain the wort and rinse the grains in a single step.

Once the wort has been collected, it is time for it to be boiled. On the whole, the wort will usually be boiled for about an hour. It is during the boil that the brewer will add hops. Hops are the seed cones of the hop plant that have been traditionally used to add flavor, aroma, and bitterness to the beer. The impact that the hops have on the beer is dictated in part on how long they are boiled, and the brewer will add different hops to the boil at different times. Generally speaking, hops added at the start of the boil will impart bitterness to the beer, hops added within the last 15 minutes will add flavor, and hops added at the end of the boil will add aroma. Not all hops are created equal, and different hops are better suited than others to each of these functions.

After the boil, the wort needs to be cooled as quickly as possible. Cooling the wort quickly causes proteins to precipitate out of the wort which will help achieve clear beer. It will also help minimize certain off-flavors that can develop. Furthermore, yeast cannot be added until the wort is a cool enough temperature.

Once the wort has been cooled to the proper temperature, the wort is transferred to a fermentation vessel. For most homebrewers, a fermentation vessel consists of either a plastic bucket or a glass carboy. Either immediately before, or immediately after, the wort is transferred to the fermentation vessel the yeast is added to the wort. This is called "pitching."

The process of boiling the wort has driven off oxygen and the wort will need to be aerated since the yeast will require oxygen at the start of fermentation. The most common way for the homebrewer to add oxygen to the wort is to vigorously shake the fermentation vessel. Other ways to aerate the wort include using an air pump or even injecting pure oxygen.

Once the yeast has been pitched and the wort has been aerated, it is time to let nature take its course. Over the next few days, fermentation will occur wherein the yeast will begin to multiply and then start to convert the sugars into alcohol. This process can take anywhere

from a few days to more than a week to complete. Once active fermentation has finished, the beer will still need to condition and depending upon style and personal preference the beer could sit in the fermentation vessel anywhere from a week to four weeks, if not longer. Some instructions will advise you to transfer your beer to a "secondary" fermenter once active fermentation is complete, but this is not always necessary. For more information, see "To Secondary or Not to Secondary" on page 148.

Although what the brewer now has can properly be called beer, it is flat and it needs to be carbonated and packaged for consumption. Traditionally, the homebrewer has bottled his beer by transferring the now fermented liquid into a bottling bucket, which is usually nothing more than a 5-gallon bucket with a spigot near the bottom. A small amount of "priming" sugar is mixed into it before the beer is drained into bottles. There is still active yeast in the beer, and the yeast will convert the priming sugar into alcohol. A by-product of fermentation is carbon dioxide. In a capped bottle there is no place for the carbon dioxide to escape to and it will dissolve into the beer. After another week or two, the brewer will have carbonated beer that is ready to be enjoyed.

EXTRACT BREWING IS the simplest place to start for your first brew. While many people who stay with the hobby will move on to partial-mash and all-grain brewing, there are just as many who will continue to brew with extracts. Extract brewing is less equipment-intensive and takes less time on brew day. Furthermore, it is not unheard of for extract brews to place in competition, demonstrating that great beer can be brewed from extracts.

When brewing with extracts, you have left the extract manufac-turer to perform the mash for you. They go through the same process

② EXTRACT BREWING

that a homebrewer would use to extract the complex carbohydrate starches from the grain and then convert those starches into sugars. The extract manufacturer will start with malted barley, perform a mash, and then collect the wort. At this point, instead of taking the further steps necessary to turn the wort into beer, the extract manufacturer will either condense the liquid into liquid malt extract or dehydrate it to make dried malt extract. This is where the extract homebrewer steps in.

During the process of extract brewing, one of the first steps that the homebrewer takes is to rehydrate the extract by adding water back into it, creating wort. The wort is then boiled for about an hour on average, and hops are added at various times during the boil in order to add bitterness, flavor, and aroma. The timing of the hop additions will determine what effect the hops will have on the final product. Bittering hops will be added early in the boil, while flavor and aroma hops will be added at, or near, the end of the boil. The wort is then cooled as rapidly as possible, after which yeast is added to the cool wort and it is allowed to ferment. The fermentation process can take anywhere from a few days to a few weeks, and after fermentation is finished it is preferable to allow the beer to condition a bit before bottling.

During fermentation, yeast and other sediment will settle to the bottom of the fermentation vessel. This sediment at the bottom of the fermentation vessel is called "trub" (rhymes with *tube*). If you are fermenting in a glass carboy, you will be able to see the sediment at the bottom of the carboy, which can be an inch or more in depth. Once you are ready to bottle, the beer will be siphoned off the yeast and other sediment into the bottling bucket and gently mixed with some priming sugar. Once the beer has been bottled, residual yeast will act upon this sugar creating carbon dioxide (CO_2). Since the bottle has

been capped at this point, the CO_2 cannot escape and dissolves back into the beer, carbonating it.

There are two general types of extracts used by homebrewers, dried malt extract (DME) and liquid malt extract (LME). Use of one or the other is usually a matter of preference and one can be substituted for the other in a recipe with some modification (see the sidebar "Recipe Conversions"). When purchasing malt extract, there are usually a number of choices based on "color." The usual choices are "light" and "dark," but you can sometimes find extracts labeled as "amber," "gold," or "extra dark." If the recipe you are following does not specifically state which color to use, you can usually presume that the recipe calls for light malt extract.

Recipe Conversions

Any recipe that you find on the web or in a book can be converted from all-grain to extract or from dried to liquid extract (or vice versa).

When a recipe calls for the use of DME, you will need to use approximately 20 percent more LME to get the same results.

All-grain brewers measure their efficiency at extracting starches from the grain, and then in converting those starches into sugars. This measurement is called brew-house efficiency. When a recipe is printed in a book or posted on the Internet there are assumptions being made about the brewer's efficiency—most often the brewhouse efficiency is assumed to be 65 percent.

When the brew-house efficiency is assumed to be 65 percent, one pound of grain needs to be replaced with approximately 0.6 lbs. of DME, or 0.75 lbs. of LME.

Another thing to keep in mind when purchasing extracts is that liquid extracts often come in "hopped" and "unhopped" varieties. If the package does not indicate one way or the other, you can assume that it is the unhopped variety. You will find that most recipes call for unhopped malt extract. The selection and addition of hops is one of the primary places where extract brewers have an opportunity to tweak recipes to taste and personal preference.

PHOTO COURTESY OF BROOKLYN HOMEBREW

ABOVE: All of the equipment needed for your first time homebrewing can be found at your local homebrew store.

The Equipment

As as mentioned before, one of the benefits of brewing with extracts is that it requires a relatively minimal amount of equipment. At its simplest, you will need the following special equipment.

- **Large pot.** You will need a large pot in order to boil the wort. It should be at least 4 gallons but a large pot of up to 7–8 gallons is preferable. During your brew session you are going to need to boil the wort for approximately 60 minutes and you ideally want to boil as large a volume as possible. Furthermore, you are going to lose some volume to evaporation. If you are brewing 5

gallons of beer you may need to start out with 6 gallons of liquid to compensate for the evaporation. *It is OK if your pot is not large enough to hold the entire volume of liquid. You can add water at the end if necessary.*

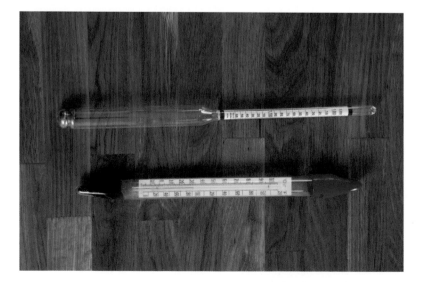

ABOVE: A hydrometer and a thermometer. The ability to take precise measurements goes a long way toward making good beer.

- **Floating thermometer.** At various points during the brewing session you will need to know temperature. Whether you are measuring the temp of the water before the boil, or of the wort afterward, a good floating thermometer is an absolute necessity.
- **Nylon mesh or muslin bag.** Most ingredient kits come with a selection of specialty grains that need to be steeped in hot water. You will use either a nylon mesh bag or a muslin bag to hold the grains so that they can be easily removed from the water when done. A nylon mesh bag has the advantage of being reusable.
- **Fermenter.** This will simply be either a 6.5-gallon food-grade bucket with a lid or a glass carboy that you will use to ferment your beer in.
- **Stirring spoon.** You will want a large spoon to stir the wort as it boils.
- **Airlock.** This is a small piece of plastic that is used to seal the fermenter and keep bacteria and oxygen out, while allowing the

BELOW: Airlocks are nothing more than pieces of plastic that hold a small amount of water (blue in the picture), allowing gasses to escape, without allowing air to enter the fermenter.

A wort chiller is an effective way to quickly cool your wort.

CO_2 caused by fermentation to escape. It sounds complicated and impressive but is actually quite simple.

- **Sanitizer.** Everything needs to be kept clean and free of unwanted bacteria. See page 29 for further discussion regarding sanitizers.

The following are handy to have, although not strictly necessary.

- **Hydrometer.** A hydrometer is used to measure specific gravity based on how high the hydrometer floats in a liquid. In dense liquid the hydrometer floats high, but will sink further down as the liquid becomes less dense. As your beer ferments it will get less dense as sugars are fermented into alcohol, and you can use this to track the progress of the fermentation. You can also use a hydrometer to estimate alcohol content by looking at the difference in the hydrometer readings before and after fermentation.
- **5-Gallon bucket.** An extra bucket is good to have around. It is useful to keep the bucket filled with sanitizer and at hand during the course of brewing.
- **Wort chiller.** The most common type of wort chiller available to the homebrewer consists of a length of copper tubing that is immersed in the hot wort. Cold water from the faucet is run through the tube and draws off the heat, effectively cooling the wort.

Once you have brewed and fermented your beer, you will need the following equipment to bottle your beer. Bottling will be covered in the following chapter, but it is a good idea to make sure that you have the equipment you need to bottle now.

- **6.5-Gallon bucket**. You will need a second bucket to use as a bottling bucket; one with a spigot at the bottom is preferable. You cannot use the same bucket you used as a fermenter because you will need to siphon the beer from the fermenter into the second bucket.

Hydrometers

If your basic brewing kit came with a hydrometer, you will want to take a hydrometer reading once you have added enough water to bring you to your target volume. The hydrometer probably came in a clear plastic tube, and you are going to fill that tube about halfway with wort. A handy device used to collect the wort is called a wine thief. There are a couple of different types of wine thieves, but they all allow you to easily remove a sample of the wort from not only the brew pot but also from the fermentation buckets and carboys. Some wine thieves allow you to take the hydrometer reading directly in the thief without having to transfer the wort to the clear plastic tube that the hydrometer came in. As an alternative, if you are bucket fermenting, the hydrometer can be floated directly in the bucket.

Once you have your sample ready, place the hydrometer in the sample. (The bulb goes into the wort, while the long thin stem will stick out of the wort.) The hydrometer will float, and depending upon the specific gravity of the sample it will float higher or lower. There are usually three different scales on the hydrometer. The scale for potential alcohol is not useful to homebrewers as it is calibrated for wine. The two remaining scales, Specific Gravity and Plato/Brix are useful for brewing. Homebrewers by and large use the Specific Gravity reading, while Plato/Brix are primarily used by commercial brewers.

Taking a hydrometer reading will allow you to determine the alcohol content of your beer and to properly determine when the beer is done fermenting. Once all visible fermentation activity has stopped, you take multiple hydrometer readings over a number of days. When the hydrometer reading is stable for two or three days, you can rest assured that fermentation is complete.

In order to determine the alcohol content, you will need to know both the original and final gravity readings. You plug the numbers into the following equation, where your initial gravity reading before fermentation is OG, and the final gravity reading after fermentation is complete is FG.

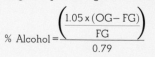

$$\% \text{ Alcohol} = \frac{\left(\frac{1.05 \times (\text{OG} - \text{FG})}{\text{FG}} \right)}{0.79}$$

A bench capper.

- **Siphon hose.** Used to siphon the beer from the fermenter to the bottling bucket. At this point in the process you want to avoid mixing in air (which will cause the beer to go stale), and you want to leave the trub in the bottom of the fermenter. Accordingly, you cannot pour the beer out of the fermenter into the bottling bucket.

- **Bottles.** Bottles can be obtained from a homebrew store, or it is possible to reuse bottles from commercial beers. If you are going to reuse commercial beer bottles you need to make sure that they are crown tops (the kind that require a bottle opener), not twist-off bottles. You will need approximately two cases of 12-ounce bottles (48 total) to hold 5 gallons of beer. It is a good idea to have a few extra in case you have enough beer for an extra bottle or two.

- **Capper.** Once you get the beer into the bottles you will need a way to attach the bottle caps. There are two styles available. Wing cappers and bench cappers. Wing cappers are less expensive and thus are a good choice when first starting out. Cappers work by crimping the cap around the top of the bottle.

- **Bottle caps.** There are two types available: standard and ones that have an oxygen absorbing lining. Either type is fine.

The following items are nice to have and will make bottling a lot easier, but are not absolutely necessary.

- **Racking cane.** A racking cane is a rigid plastic tube that is attached to your siphon hose. It usually has a plastic piece at the end that will hold the cane up off the bottom of the fermenter to keep the trub from being siphoned along with the beer.

- **Auto-siphon.** An alternative to a racking cane is an auto-siphon. The most common one found is made by a company named Fermtech. It allows you to start a siphon without using your mouth or water to get it started. If you don't buy this for your first brew, you should definitely buy it for your second.

- **Bottle filler.** This is a rigid piece of plastic tube with either a gravity-operated or spring-loaded valve. You attach this to the

ABOVE: Two types of bottle fillers: the one on the left with the black tip uses the pressure of the beer coming out of the bottling bucket to close the valve at its tip; the other one uses a spring.

spigot of your bottling bucket with a piece of flexible tube. You place it into your bottle, and press the tip against the bottom of the bottle which causes the beer to start to flow, filling the bottle from the bottom to help avoid aeration. When you lift the tip off of the bottom, the beer stops flowing.

- **Bottle brush.** It is difficult to list this in the "not necessary" section, as it may be necessary to clean out used commercial bottles. But you can get away without it, if you are using brand-new bottles, or if you are extremely selective in the bottles you save for homebrewing use.

Many homebrew stores have starter kits that will have most of the equipment you need to get started. These kits usually contain the buckets used to ferment and bottle the beer, airlocks, thermometer, hydrometer, siphon hoses, racking cane, and a capper. They may or may not contain sanitizer and they will almost never include the large pot and the bottles.

The Ingredients

Most homebrew stores will also have basic ingredient kits available. These are usually marketed as clones of famous beers or will at the very least give the ingredients for a specific style of beer. They usually contain the malt extract, specialty grains, hops, and yeast necessary for a given recipe. They will also have rudimentary instructions on how to brew the kit, and will often include the bottle caps and sometimes a muslin bag to hold the specialty grains during steeping. For a novice brewer, these kits are an excellent place to start and are highly recommended for at least your first brew if not your first few brews.

Cleaning and Sanitization

Homebrew sessions always start and end the same way, with cleaning. While it is admittedly one of my least favorite parts of the process, in many ways it is one of the most important. The entire process of brewing is geared toward creating the perfect environment for brewing yeast to thrive, and this means that wild yeast and bacteria will thrive as well. The way to prevent this is with careful cleaning and sanitization.

At the outset, you want to make sure that all of your equipment has been cleaned and rinsed of any soap residue. With new equipment

you are concerned with oils and solvents left over from the manufac-
turing process, as well as any dirt and dust that the equipment picked
up during transportation. With old equipment (i.e., equipment you
already have or someone else has already used) you want to make sure
that the old brew doesn't make its way into the new one.

Sanitization starts with cleaning. You can soak the equipment
in the sanitizer of your choice for as long as you like, and it will be
for naught if you don't start with clean equipment. Bacteria and wild
yeast can hide from the sanitizer beneath dirt and grime, only to
come back to haunt you later on. If all of your equipment is clean at
the start of the brewing process, it will make everything easier going
forward.

Once you are confident your equipment is clean it is time to think
about sanitization. Prior to the boil, your equipment just needs to be
clean, as the heat of the boiling process sanitizes the wort. It takes
about 15 minutes of boiling to achieve a proper level of sanitization,
that means anything that comes into contact with the wort when there
is less than 15 minutes of boiling left needs to be sanitized.

If you are using a commercial sanitizer, follow the manufacturer's instructions. The nice part about many commercial sanitizers
sold for the purpose of homebrewing is that they are "no-rinse" sanitizers. This means that it is OK to allow an object with sanitizer on it
to come into contact with the wort/beer. It will not affect the flavor or
its ability to ferment. Some commercial sanitizers have a tendency
to foam up when agitated. It is also OK to allow the foam to come into
contact, and even get into, the wort/beer.

It is a good idea to take a spare 5-gallon bucket and half fill it
with sanitizer. This is a good place to put equipment down when you
are not using it. As an example, after you stir the wort you will most
likely want to put your stirring spoon down (unless you intend to hold
it for the rest of the process). Putting it into the bucket of sanitizer is
a great place to leave it, along with siphon hoses, airlocks, and pretty
much anything else that will fit in the bucket of sanitizer.

If you do not have a commercial sanitizer, you can use household bleach. Bleach can be a powerful sanitizer and a little will go a long way. As a general rule of thumb, you can use one teaspoon of bleach mixed with one gallon of water. While bleach can be used successfully as a sanitizer, there are two potential downsides to bleach. The first is that bleach has the potential to cause a medicinal flavor in beer. As such it is recommended that you rinse off an item that has been sanitized with bleach before it comes into contact with your

BELOW: A spare bucket filled with sanitizer is a good place to put your equipment down while you're brewing.

wort/beer, and unless you are rinsing with boiled water, rinsing has the potential to reintroduce contaminants. The other is that bleach has the potential to corrode stainless steel, if the pH of the solution gets too low. Not necessarily a problem, but something to keep in mind.

The Process

West Coast IPA

The following is a recipe for an American version of an IPA (India Pale Ale). It is heavy on hop character, using hops often found in West Coast beers. It uses a characteristically clean yeast that allows the hop flavor to dominate with hints of grapefruit and a full floral aroma.

9.3 lbs. Pale LME (or 7.5 lbs. of Pale DME)

1 lb. Caramel/Crystal Malt 40 Lovibond

1 oz. Simcoe Hops (60 minute boil)
1 oz. Amarillo Gold Hops (15 minute boil)
1 oz. Amarillo Gold Hops (flame out)

Wyeast 1056 American Ale yeast

Original Gravity 1.068
Final Gravity Estimate 1.017

International Bitterness Units (IBU) 54.6

1. Yeast

Depending on the type of yeast that you are using, you may need to start preparing your yeast a few days ahead of time. There are two types of yeast that you will come across, liquid and dry. If you are using dry yeast, all you need to do is sprinkle the yeast into about a cup of warm water 15–20 minutes before you pitch the yeast into your wort.

If you are using liquid yeast, however, in most cases it will require that you make a starter a few days ahead of time. Detailed instructions on creating a starter can be found in chapter 9 on yeast, but it essentially entails pitching the yeast into a small volume of wort. This wort is almost always made with malt extract, even if you are brewing an all-grain beer. The advantages to using a starter are twofold. First the yeast starts to reproduce, so you will be able to pitch a greater amount of yeast than you would otherwise. Second, you are ensuring that the yeast is viable. Both go a long way toward an active and healthy fermentation.

For the West Coast IPA on page 32, make a 1-liter starter at least two days prior to brewing.

2. Clean

It is worth repeating: the first step on brew day is to clean all of your equipment and then to sanitize and keep sanitized anything that will come into contact with the wort after it has been boiled.

3. Specialty Grains

If your kit or recipe uses specialty grains, you will need to steep these in hot water first. While not all recipes use specialty grains, there are far more kits and recipes out there that use them than there are that don't. While it is an extra step in the process, it is almost as simple as making a cup of tea. If you are making the West Coast IPA you are going to steep the pound of Crystal Malt found in the recipe.

Start by bringing about 2.5 gallons of water to 170 degrees Fahrenheit.

While your water is coming to temp, you need to determine if the grains have been crushed or not. You can easily tell by looking: If the barley grains are whole and round, they have not been crushed. If they are broken up into pieces, they have been crushed. It is obviously easier if the grains have been pre-crushed, and most retailers

ABOVE: Using a rolling pin to crush grains.

will give you the option to have them crushed or not. If you're given the option, have them crushed.

If they have not been crushed, take the grain and place it into a plastic bag (a large resealable bag is great for this) and go over it with a rolling pin. If you do not have a rolling pin, you can use a glass beer bottle laid on its side. While you will not achieve the same level of crush that you would with a grain mill, you can get acceptable results using this method. You want to make sure that the grains have at least been cracked open.

Once you have crushed grains, place the grain in either a nylon mesh or muslin bag. When the water has come to 170 degrees Fahrenheit, take the water off heat and place the grains into the water. Let it steep for 20 minutes—just like making tea—and then remove the grains from the water. You will notice during this part of the process that the water begins to take on some of the color of the grain.

ABOVE: As the specialty grains steep, the water will begin to take on some of their color and flavor.

4. Start the Boil and Add the Extract

Once the specialty grains have been removed, bring the water to a boil and add approximately a pound of extract for every gallon of water that you are boiling. When working with extracts there is no need to do a full boil, or to boil all of the extract for a full hour, as you would do with all-grain brewing. The company that prepared the extract went to all of the trouble of performing a full boil before reducing the wort to extract. While you can boil the full amount if you want to, and you will find a lot of recipes that call for a full boil, it is not necessary. Boiling the full amount of extracts may cause some darkening of the wort and could mildly affect the final flavor of the beer. This is

more of concern when making light-flavored and colored beers such as pale ales, but less of a concern when brewing darker fuller-bodied beers like stouts and porters.

A note about boiling: When boiling wort, there is always the possibility of a boilover. This can be avoided by routinely stirring the wort. Boilovers are a very messy event. The wort is very sweet and sticky and when there is a boilover, as you could guess, your stove will now be very sticky. Boilovers are most likely to happen when the wort first comes to a boil and when you add anything to the boiling wort such as hops. Which brings us to the next step.

5. Add the Bittering Hops

Different characteristics will be extracted from hops depending on when they are added to the wort. Hops that are going to be used for their bitter characteristic are added at the start of the boil and will usually be boiled for 60 minutes. Other hops will be added near the end of the boil for aroma and flavor characteristics. You can add the hops directly to the wort.

Your recipe should indicate which hops are going to be used for bittering. It is possible that the same type of hop or multiple types of hops will be used for both bittering and flavor additions, in which case your recipe will tell you how much of the hops are to be used at the start of the boil. If you are following the IPA recipe (see page 32), you should add the one ounce of Simcoe hops at this time.

6. Add Flavor Hops and the Remaining Extract

After 45 minutes (with 15 minutes left on the boil) you will add the hops that have been chosen for their flavor characteristics. As with the bittering hops, they can be added directly to the boiling wort. Any remaining extract should be added, and boiled for a full 15 minutes. In the IPA recipe, you will want to add one ounce of Amarillo hops and the remaining malt extract.

7. The End of the Boil/Aroma Hops

After 60 minutes you can remove the wort from heat and bring the boil to an end. Your recipe may (or may not) call for a third hop addition, with hops that have been chosen for their aroma characteristics; these can also be added directly to the wort. In the West Coast IPA recipe mentioned above, you would add the remaining ounce of Amarillo Hops.

If you have been paying attention, you might wonder if the hops need to be sanitized as they are being added to the wort after the boil has been finished. They do not, as hops have a natural antibacterial quality to them. They are actually used in part to help preserve the beer, so they can be added to the wort without worry. That being said, everything else that will come into contact with your wort must be sanitized from this point forward, including the spoon that you will use to stir the hops into the wort.

8. Chill

Once you take the wort off of the heat source, you will want to cool the wort down as quickly as possible. The easiest way to do this is to place the pot into an ice bath. You can do this in your sink, or if the pot doesn't fit in your sink you can use your bathtub or a large plastic storage container.

ABOVE: A submersion chiller is placed into the wort and cold water is run through it in order to bring the temperature of the wort down.

As indicated, you want to bring the temperature of the wort down as quickly as possible. Make sure that you are using a mix of ice and water, as this will cool the wort down faster than ice alone. Occasionally, you will want to stir or agitate the ice bath as the water closest to the pot warms up. Your goal is to get the temperature down to 70 degrees Fahrenheit, if not lower. Remember to sanitize your thermometer.

Another option is the use of a submersion chiller. Submersion chillers usually consist of a coil of copper pipe that is submerged in the wort. Cold water is run through the pipe quickly cooling the wort down.

9. Pitch

Once the temperature of the wort has gotten down to 70 degrees Fahrenheit or below, it is time to add the yeast to the wort. Pour the yeast directly into the wort and stir. If you have used a starter, you can add the entire starter, or if the starter has settled, you can decant the liquid off of the yeast and pitch only the yeast. (See page 156 for detailed information on starters.)

10. Final Steps

At this point, the brewing process is done, and it is time to let the yeast do its job and ferment the beer. If you are using a bucket as a

fermentation vessel, pour the wort into your sanitized bucket so that it splashes around a bit. The yeast requires oxygen and by causing the wort to splash you are effectively aerating it. For good measure, you could pour the wort back into the boiling pot, and back again into the bucket a few times to ensure that it is well aerated.

If you are using a glass (or plastic) carboy, you will need to siphon the wort into the carboy as the opening is not nearly as big as the opening on a plastic bucket. (Once again make sure that the siphon hose and the carboy have been sanitized.) Once the wort is in the carboy, you need to cap off the top of the carboy using a rubber stopper. In order to

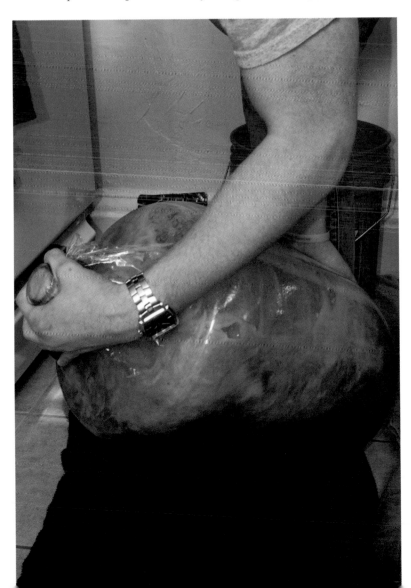

aerate it, tilt the carboy on its edge (see the accompanying picture) and rock the carboy back and forth vigorously for about 5 minutes.

The final step is to add water to the fermentation vessel to achieve a total of 5 gallons of wort. You started the process by bringing approximately 2.5 gallons of water to a boil, and you have lost some volume to

evaporation. You can add water directly from your sink. While there is a small concern of contamination, the fact is that if your water is good enough for you to drink from the tap, it will probably be just fine for you to add to the fermenter at the end of the brewing session. Some people do this step as part of the chilling phase. The addition of cold water can help you quickly bring the temperature of the wort down.

If you are using a plastic bucket as a fermenter, you can just put the lid on the bucket and put the bucket aside in a cool location for the next two weeks while fermentation takes place. If you purchased a basic equipment kit, the bucket lid may have come with a hole in it for you to place an airlock. Either way is fine. If you are using a carboy, you will need to use an airlock with a rubber stopper. Place a small amount of water or sanitizer in the airlock to prevent air and bacteria from making its way down into the fermenter.

Fermentation will take at least two weeks to complete. There is nothing to do at this point but wait, and clean your equipment.

(3)
BOTTLING

AFTER FERMENTATION IS complete, it is time to bottle your beer. You want to make sure that fermentation is fully complete; otherwise you can run into problems resulting from over-carbonated beer. Ideally, you will take hydrometer readings near the end of fermentation over the course of a few days to make sure that the reading has stabilized. Once you get the same reading three days in a row you should be safe. If you don't have a hydrometer you should definitely wait a full two weeks before bottling. While not fail safe, you can be fairly certain that fermentation is done.

Bottling involves not only getting your beer into bottles, but also adding a small amount of sugar to the beer. The remaining yeast in the beer will act upon this sugar to create CO_2. Since the bottle is capped there is no place for the CO_2 to go, and it dissolves into the beer, creating carbonation.

The equipment needed to bottle was covered in the previous chapter on extract brewing (see page 19), but in short you will need the following items.

- **6.5-Gallon bucket**. One with a spigot at the bottom is preferable. You cannot use the same bucket that you used as a fermenter because you will need to siphon the beer from the fermenter into the second bucket.

- **Siphon hose.** Used to siphon the beer from the fermenter to the bottling bucket.
- **Bottles.** You will need approximately two cases (48 total) of 12-ounce bottles to hold 5 gallons of beer.

- **Capper.** Used to affix the caps to the bottles.
- **Bottle caps.**

The following items make bottling easier, but are not absolutely necessary.

- **Racking cane.** A racking cane is a piece of rigid plastic tube that is attached to your siphon hose.
- **Auto siphon.** An alternative to a racking cane is an auto-siphon. It allows you to easily start a siphon.
- **Bottle filler.** You attach this to the spigot of your bottling bucket and use it to control the flow of beer into the bottle.
- **Bottle brush.** To clean your bottles.

The Process

1. Clean and Sanitize

As stated in the last chapter, most activities start with cleaning and sanitizing your equipment. You want to make sure that your buckets, hoses, bottle fillers, racking canes, bottles, and caps are all clean and sanitized.

If you are reusing old bottles, you may want to start the cleaning process a few days early. Soak the bottles in a sodium precarbonate cleaner such as OxiClean or PBW for one to two days. Allowing the bottles to soak in a water and cleaner solution will get rid of most dirt and beer residue without the necessity of mechanical removal (i.e., scrubbing) and has the added benefit of making the labels easy to remove. Use one scoop of OxiClean in a large garbage can filled with about 15 gallons of water. If space is a concern, you can also do smaller batches in a spare bucket. This will take care of most bottles, but see additional methods in chapter 5 on cleaning and sanitizing.

Start the sanitization process by filling your bottling bucket half way with a sanitizer solution. Agitate and rinse the bottling bucket with the solution, and then pour the sanitizer into a spare bucket. Sanitize the rest of your equipment and keep it in the solution in the spare bucket until you are ready to use it.

Your bottles will need to be sanitized too. They can either be sanitized as you bottle or all sanitized in advance. If you are sanitizing as you bottle, submerge several bottles in the bucket of sanitizer and leave them there until you need them. When you take one bottle out to fill with beer, replace it with another; this is easier to do if you have help. If you decide to sanitize all of your bottles in advance, cover each one with a piece of sanitized aluminum foil until you need it. Remove the aluminum foil right before you fill the bottle. This is often the easier method if you are bottling alone.

The easiest thing to do with bottle caps is to simply soak the bottle caps in a bowl of sanitizer. You will find references in some older material that recommends boiling the caps for 10 to 15 minutes and then allowing them to cool while you bottle. This method works in a

pinch, but there are some reports that it can damage the lining of the bottle caps and prevent them from sealing properly.

2. Prepare Your Priming Sugar

Priming sugar is used to carbonate your beer. Although most of the yeast has fallen out of suspension (which you can see in the upper layers of the sediment on the bottom of your fermentation vessel), there is still quite a lot of yeast left in the beer. As mentioned, this remaining yeast acts on the priming sugar to create CO_2, and the sealed cap prevents the CO_2 from escaping. Over a period of days the CO_2 dissolves into the beer, creating carbonation.

Generally speaking, you will want to use about 4 ounces of corn sugar for 5 gallons of beer. Ideally you measure your priming sugar by weight, as it is the only way to ensure consistency. If you do not have the ability to measure by weight, 4 ounces of corn sugar is approximately ¾ cup by volume.

You can also use dried malt extract, by using approximately 1¼ cups. This is similar to how some breweries bottle carbonate, where they hold back a portion of the wort to be added at the time of bottling.

The advantage to using corn sugar is that it will carbonate the beer faster than by using malt extract. Corn sugar will take approximately two weeks to properly carbonate your beer, while malt extract may take twice as long.

It is important to realize that this is a general guideline. Technically, different styles call for different levels of carbonation. But 4 ounces of corn sugar will put you somewhere in the middle of the different carbonation levels.

Whether you are using corn sugar or malt extract, bring 1 cup of water to a

RIGHT: Boiling your priming sugar both sanitizes it and makes it easier to fully dissolve it into the beer.

boil, and dissolve the priming sugar into it. Boil for 5–10 minutes and then allow it to cool while you set up to rack your beer.

3. Racking

Generally speaking, racking is the process of moving your beer from one container to another. When racking for bottling you are removing your beer from the sediment at the bottom of your fermenting vessel. If you have used a clear vessel—such as a glass carboy—you can see sediment at the bottom, but even if you can't see it you can be certain that it is there.

The trick is to remove as much of the beer as possible without disturbing the sediment, and thereby keeping the sediment out of your bottling bucket. A racking cane is ideal for this, as they usually have a piece of plastic on one end which lifts the end of the cane up off the bottom and out of the sediment. The other end of the cane is attached to a hose which completes the siphon.

Since a siphon works off of gravity, you will need to place the fermentation vessel up higher than the bottling bucket. The usual method is to place the fermentation vessel on a counter or tabletop, and place the bottling bucket on the floor. If your bottling bucket has a spigot on it, the spigot likely protrudes below the bottom of the bucket but can be rotated up so that the bucket can rest evenly on the floor. The siphon hose should be able to reach all the way to the bottom of the bottling bucket to avoid splashing that aerates the beer. At this stage in the process, you want to avoid aerating the beer as much as possible. If too much aeration takes place, the beer will become oxidized and go stale much more quickly. Once the beer has started to flow into the bottling bucket, you will want to keep the bottom of the siphon hose submerged to prevent splashing and agitation that will lead to aeration.

There are a number of methods to getting the siphon started. If you have an auto-siphon, simply follow the instructions that came with it. If you do not have an auto-siphon you'll have to start it manually. For rather obvious sanitation reasons, it is not recommended that you use your mouth. Instead, fill the siphon hose with water, and

A bottling bucket spigot rotated up so that it doesn't hit the surface that the bucket is sitting on. When it's time to bottle, hang the spigot over the edge of the surface, and rotate the spigot down into position.

4 Gallon

3 Gallon

2 Gallon

1 Gallon

pinch off the lower end so that the water does not flow out of it. Place the racking cane end into the beer and lower the siphon hose end into the bottling bucket and release the water. The water flowing out of the hose and into the bottling bucket will start the siphon. It is OK to use tap water for this, although some people use either boiled water or sanitizer.

Just as the siphon starts, add the priming sugar that you prepared earlier to the bottling bucket. You will use the force of the beer being siphoned into the bottling bucket to start mixing the priming sugar into the beer. Remember to keep the end of the siphon hose submerged as much as possible to avoid aeration. Once you have siphoned all of the beer into the bottling bucket, you will need to gently (without splashing), but thoroughly, stir the beer with a clean and sanitized spoon to ensure that the priming sugar has fully mixed with the beer.

4. Bottling

Once the beer has been racked from the fermentation vessel to the bottling bucket, you will want to move the bottling bucket onto

a table or other raised surface. Rotate the spigot so that it is facing
down and hanging off the edge of the table. Attach your bottle filler
to the spigot with a short piece of hose.

Take your first clean and sanitized bottle and place the bottle
filler in the bottle so that the tip of the bottle filler is pressing against

the bottle bottom. Turn the bottling bucket spigot on so that beer begins to flow into the bottle. When the beer gets close to the top of the mouth of the bottle, pull the bottle slightly down so that the bottle filler lifts off of the bottom; this will cause the beer to stop flowing into the bottle. Turn the bottling bucket spigot off, and pull the bottle filler out of the bottle. While the bottle filler was in the bottle, it was displacing some beer. As the bottle filler is removed, the level of the beer in the bottle should drop about halfway down the neck of the bottle.

The level will vary a bit from bottle to bottle,
but aim to fill to about the middle of the neck.

5. Capping

Once you have filled a half a dozen bottles or so, you can start to cap them. There are two types of cappers available, bench cappers and wing cappers. Most basic brewing kits come with a wing capper. Place a bottle cap on top of the bottle, and lower the capper on top. Slowly bring the "wings" of the capper down. As the wings rotate down, the capper will grab the neck of the bottle and crimp the cap onto the crown top. When using a bench capper, you begin by placing the bottle on the base of the capper and a cap on top of the bottle. As you draw the lever down, the capping mechanism descends and presses the cap onto the bottle. Bench cappers are often adjustable, allowing you to cap different sized bottles. Bench cappers can also cap twist-off-type bottles and other bottles that lack the ridge at the top of the neck that is required by crown cappers.

Using a Bench Capper.

6. Waiting and Cleaning

Once you have capped the entire batch of beer, there is nothing to do but put the filled bottles someplace dark and out of the way, clean your equipment, and wait. Sitting at room temperature, it will take about two weeks for your beer to properly carbonate. Avoid placing the uncarbonated beer in a refrigerator or keeping it in a cold area of the house. While your beer will carbonate at cooler temperatures, it can take much longer.

7. Serving

After about two weeks, your beer will be ready to serve. You want to avoid drinking homebrew (or any other bottle-conditioned beer) out of the bottle. At the bottom of every bottle-conditioned beer is a layer of yeast. When you serve a homebrew, slowly pour the beer from the bottle, trying not to disturb the yeast sediment at the bottom.

If you do get yeast into the glass you can still drink it, but it's better to avoid for a variety of reasons. First, it can be unsightly in the glass. It looks like little gobs of goo, floating around in the beer. Some people will find it a turnoff and not want to drink the beer. Too much yeast in the glass and the beer will tasty bready. Finally, there is also the problem that it can cause flatulence.

Bottle Choices

Obviously, if you are going to bottle your beer you will need a supply of bottles, and there are many choices. If you are going to purchase new bottles from a homebrew supplier, you will have a choice of size and type of closure. The most common sizes of bottles are the 12-ounce and the larger 22-ounce bottles (also known as bombers). Twelve-ounce bottles are the standard bottle type that you are used to seeing in a six-pack. Twenty-two-ounce bottles are the larger bottles that craft beers are often sold in. The obvious advantage to 22-ounce bottles is that, since they hold more, you have to clean, sanitize, fill, and cap fewer bottles. The drawback is that when your beer is pack-

A flip-top bottle.

aged in 22-ounce bottles there are fewer of them to share, and you are committed to drinking a larger amount of beer when you open one. You can also find bottles in 16 and 32 ounces and the 750-milliliter size that some Belgian beers come in.

You also have a choice in the type of closure: crown top or swing top. The crown-top bottle is the type of bottle that you place a bottle cap on. The caps are single use, and require a capper to put on. Swing-top closures are the type of closure that Grolsch Lager is traditionally sold in. They are so often identified with Grolsch that they are often called Grolsch-style caps, but may also be known as flip-top caps. They can be put on by hand and are reusable, although the rubber gasket that creates the seal between the top and the bottle will

need to be occasionally replaced. Either style is fine to use, but you
need to remember that they are not interchangeable (i.e., you can't
use a swing-style closure on a crown-top bottle and vice versa), and
the swing-top closure bottles often cost more than twice the price of
crown-top bottles.

Many homebrewers reuse commercial beer bottles. When choosing commercial beer bottles to use for homebrew, there are a couple
of things that you want to take into consideration. The first is that you
want to make sure that you obtain a dark-colored bottle. While you
might think a clear bottle will be nice to show off your homemade
beer, clear glass is less than an ideal choice for beer. Dark-colored
glass protects the beer from light, which can spoil beer. "Light-
struck" beer develops off-flavors, and is what happened to a beer that
has been "skunked." Obviously, the darker the glass, the better protection that is afforded the beer—brown is preferable to green, which
is preferable to clear.

You also need to pay attention to the type of closure on the bottle. Many commercial beers come in twist-off bottles, avoiding the

BELOW: A crown-top bottle; notice the lower ridge that a wing capper grabs onto.

obstacle of a bottle opener coming between beer and customer. While you can use a twist-off bottle with a standard crown cap, you cannot use a wing capper to cap it. You must use a bench capper. If you look at the top of a crown cap bottle, you will see that just below the lip of the bottle there is another protrusion—a second lip or ridge. A wing capper grabs onto this ridge and uses it for leverage when crimping the cap over the lip of the bottle. On a twist-off bottle, this ridge is either missing or is often very thin. If you try to use a wing capper, you will break the bottle, make a poor seal, or otherwise fail miserably.

The other thing to take into consideration when using commercial bottles is the condition of the bottles. Most beer sold in the United States is sold in one-time-use bottles. Such bottles are not meant to be reused and have thin glass, which makes them prone to damage. Damaged bottles should never be used. You particularly want to avoid using them for highly carbonated styles of beer, as the bottle may not be able to take the pressure. If ever in doubt about the condition of a bottle, don't use it.

Kegging

Another popular method of storing and serving homemade beer is kegging. Although there are a couple of options, the most popular is to use a 5-gallon Cornelius (or "corny") keg. These kegs were originally used to store and dispense fountain soda. There are two types, "ball-lock" and "pin-lock," which designates the type of connector used to attach the hoses that allow the beer to be dispensed. The ball-lock type is the most popular. Corny kegs were once very easy to find used, but are slowly becoming harder to find and the price for them has been increasing as they are no longer used by the soft drink industry.

Kegs offer a number of advantages over bottles. They are easy to fill, simply requiring the removal of a large cap at the top of the keg before filling, as opposed to the individual filling and capping of a large number of bottles. Using compressed carbon dioxide, you can force carbonate the beer. This allows the beer to be rapidly carbon-

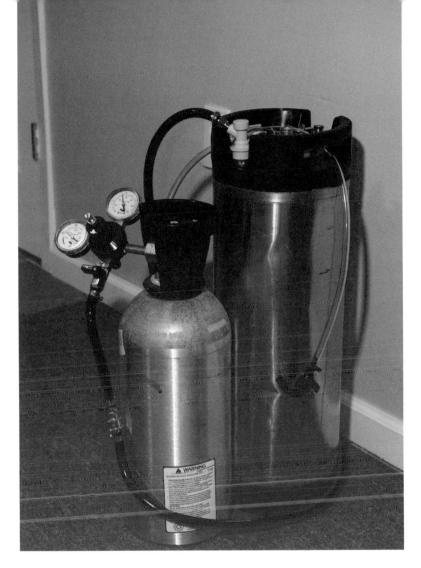

ated to a precise level of carbonation. Where natural carbonation using priming sugar can take up to two weeks, force-carbonated beer can be ready in a matter of days, if not hours.

There are a number of options when it comes to dispensing beer from a keg. The first is to chill the entire keg before use and dispense the beer through a plastic tap head, called a picnic tap, connected directly to the keg via a length of hose. Another option is to dispense through a jockey box, which is a picnic cooler or ice chest with either a stainless steel coil or channeled plate inside it through which the beer flows. The cooler is filled with ice, and as the beer flows through the coil it cools down to dispensing temperature.

ABOVE: Kegs are easy to fill after removing the lid from the top of the keg.

Finally, many people convert refrigerators and freezers into keg-
erators, which can be used to keep beer chilled, on tap, and ready to
serve. Generally, the beer is pushed out of the keg using compressed
carbon dioxide, rather than the hand pumps that you may be familiar
with. The problem with the hand pumps is that they introduce oxygen
into the keg, which causes the beer to go bad if it is not quickly consumed. With carbon dioxide, a delay serving the beer again will not
cause it to go stale.

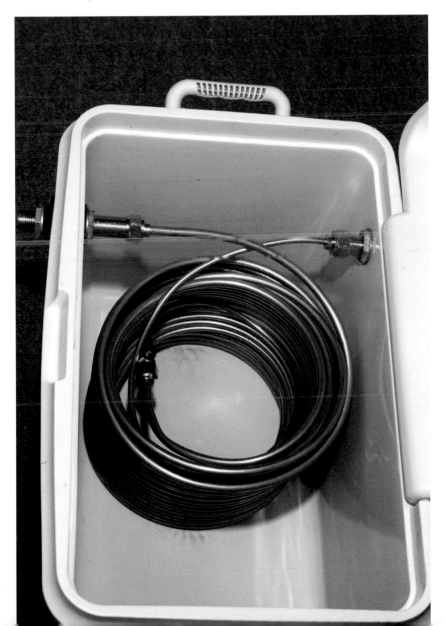

4

ALL-GRAIN AND PARTIAL-MASH BREWING

ALL-GRAIN AND PARTIAL-MASH brewing allow the home-brewer unparalleled control over the final product. Where the extract brewer relies upon the maltster to convert and extract fermentables from the grain, the all-grain and partial-mash brewer claims this process for him- or herself, and in doing so gains control over the final product that is not otherwise available. Not only does the brewer maintain full control over the final product, but these processes also open up a whole range of ingredients that cannot be obtained in extract form. While the major base malts and styles can be found in extracts, many types of specialty malts and adjuncts cannot.

The process of converting the raw material to fermentable sugar is called mashing and in itself is a fairly simple and straightforward process. The mash consists of steeping crushed grain in hot water, which causes the starches in the grain to gelatinize. This makes the starches available to enzymes that break the starches down into sugars. The sugars combine with the water to make wort. The grain is then separated from the wort, and the wort is boiled in a manner similar to extract brewing. The difference between all-grain and partial-mash brewing is that the partial-mash brewer will use the mashing process to supplement and expand upon extract brewing, while the all-grain brewer generally forgoes extract altogether.

ABOVE: Since all-grain brewing usually requires a larger pot and a greater volume of liquid, a propane burner is often used as a heat source.

BELOW: The stainless steel braid at the bottom of this picnic cooler acts as a sieve that helps separate out the wort from the grain.

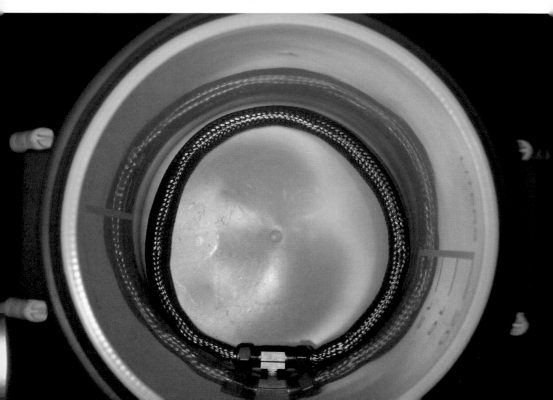

Mash Tun

The primary piece of equipment necessary to conduct a mash is a mash tun. Homebrewers often combine the mash tun with a lauter tun, which is used to separate the wort from the grain. This combined piece of equipment is referred to as an MLT. This often takes the form of a picnic cooler with a spigot at the bottom of it. The cooler insulates the mash, maintaining the mash temperature which is critical to proper starch conversion. The wort is drained from the cooler via the spigot.

A method is needed to keep the grain from flowing out of the cooler along with the wort. A manifold is sometimes placed at the bottom of the cooler to allow the water to drain and flow evenly through the grain. Another option is the use of a screen or braided stainless steel. In either case, the goal is to use the spent grain as a filter bed, clearing the wort of particulate matter as it drains through it.

A dedicated mash tun is not absolutely necessary for conducting a mash, and many work-arounds have been employed. One method is to place the grain in a large nylon bag, often sold at homebrew stores as either grain bags or strainer bags. This bag can be placed directly into the kettle or used as a strainer inside of a picnic cooler (without a manifold). This is often referred to as Brew in a Bag, and there are many devotees to the method due to its simplicity. It can be used with, and without, sparging and can be employed in brewing partial-mash or small batches of all-grain.

Milling

Prior to use, the malted barley needs to be ground or crushed. Many home-

RIGHT: Many mash/lauter tuns have built-in thermometers. This MLT has not only a thermometer, but a sight gauge that measures the volume as well.

ABOVE: Grain ready to be milled.

brew stores will gladly pre-crush the grains for you or allow you to use their mill to crush the grain yourself. This is an excellent way to get started with mashing, as it avoids the necessity of purchasing your own mill. Furthermore, you can have some assurance that the grain has been properly crushed until you have more experience with mashing and have a feel for it yourself.

The level and type of crush is extremely important to the mash process. The starch needs to be broken up in order to make it available to the mash—the smaller the pieces of grain the easier it is to convert them to sugars. Yet you do not want it ground down to flour, as it will obtain a consistency not unlike glue when you put it in water. This will make lautering (removing the grain from the wort) difficult and time consuming. The other factor to consider is the husk of the grain, as it is the husk that will form a filter bed through which the wort will be drained, effectively separating the wort from the grain. Ideally, the husk should maintain its integrity and be separated from the grain. You want to avoid tearing the husks into little pieces, as they will not make an effective filter and may add astringency to your beer.

Crushing the grain your-
self allows a level of consistency
that is not otherwise available.
The ability to extract the sugars
from the grain is dependent on
how well the grains have been
crushed and if you are relying
on someone else to crush the
grain you have no control over
this aspect of the process. Ultimately, the key to making great
beer is the ability to control
your process and the ability to
do so repeatedly.

There are two main types
of mills that are used in homebrewing. The first is the Corona-style
mill. These mills are relatively inexpensive and can be used to great
effect. The mill works by passing the grain through a set of rotat-

BELOW: A Corona mill.

ing plates. As the grains pass through, the plates crush and rip the grains apart. The drawback to this type of mill is twofold. First, they are very hard to adjust with any type of precision and they need to be adjusted often. Accordingly, the results are less than consistent. The other problem is that they tend to tear the grain husks apart, which, as mentioned previously, can negatively affect your ability to sparge and add unwanted flavors to the beer.

The other widely available type of mill is the roller mill. These mills pass the grain between two (or more) rollers, resulting in a true crush. The grain is effectively separated from the husk with a minimal amount of tearing. They are very easy to adjust, and maintain their space between the rollers giving a level of consistency that is not achievable with a Corona-style mill. The downside is that they can cost two to three times as much as a Corona-style, if not more.

BELOW: The rollers on this roller mill allow for precise control over the crush.

Efficiency

The extract potential of grain is determined by the amount of starch in the grain, and your ability to convert those starches to sugars is a measure of your efficiency. As a homebrewer, 100 percent efficiency is impossible (this can only be obtained in a laboratory using a process called a congress mash), but your efficiency can be compared to the ideal to determine how efficient your process is in converting starches to sugars and getting those sugars into the wort. Increased efficiency can be obtained by milling the grain more finely. The problem is that if the grain is ground too fine, when the wort is drained it stops acting as a filter and clogs up the entire operation making it difficult, if not impossible, to drain the wort and/or sparge water.

The Mash

In all-grain and partial-mash brewing, there are two steps in the process that have a significant impact on the outcome of the beer, fermentation and the mash. It is the conduction of a mash that separates this type of brewing from extract brewing. The mash is where the starches found in the grain are converted to sugars by enzymes found within the malted barley. The job of the brewer is to create a set of conditions that allows the enzymes to work toward the ends of the brewer. This is done by controlling the thickness of the mash, the temperature of the mash, and the amount of time that the enzymes have to do their job.

Once you have chosen a mash tun and have your grains properly crushed, it is time to start preparing the mash. The first step is to bring your strike water to the appropriate temperature. The strike water is the water that will be mixed with the grain at the start of the mash, but this raises two important questions—how much water and at what temperature?

The Science of the Mash

You can make very good beer without understanding the dynamics of the mash, but having a fuller understanding about what is taking place in the mash tun will give you the information you need to make adjustments to fit the beer to your palate. The aim of the mash is to convert the starches found within the kernel of the grain into sugars, which will be used during fermentation by the yeast to ultimately produce alcohol.

The vast majority of the barley kernel is made of starch. Starch molecules are very long chains of the simple sugar glucose. Starches are not fermentable and need to be converted to simpler sugars in order to be fermented. During the malting process a number of enzymes are developed that, under the right circumstances, will break the starches down into shorter glucose chains. These shorter chains include maltose, a very fermentable form of sugar consisting of two glucose molecules, and maltotriose, consisting of three glucose molecules, which is also fermentable. Dextrins are unfermentable chains consisting of four or more glucose molecules; while dextrins are not fermentable, they add body and mouthfeel to the beer.

There are two main enzymes that become activated during the mash, alpha-amylase and beta-amylase. Alpha-amylase is an enzyme that breaks down long chains of glucose in the middle. Beta-amylase is an enzyme that breaks apart glucose chains by breaking off molecules from the ends. Since beta-amylase works from the ends of the glucose chain, it benefits from the activity of the alpha-amylase, which by cutting the glucose chains in the middle effectively creates more ends for the beta-amylase to work with. By working together, they can quickly break down the starches into fermentable sugars.

The enzymes need to be steeped within a certain temperature range in order for them to become activated. Each enzyme works best within different temperature ranges, but there is enough overlap within the acceptable ranges to make it work. Alpha-amylase works best between 149 and 153 degrees Fahrenheit. While it will continue to work at higher temperatures, if it will become denatured (a fancy way of saying it will stop working) within two hours if the temperature exceeds 153 degrees Fahrenheit. Beta-amylase works best between 126 and 146 degrees Fahrenheit, but will become denatured within an hour at temperatures greater than 149 degrees Fahrenheit. As indicated, they will work outside of these temperature ranges, but only for a limited amount of time.

Generally speaking, both enzymes will work well together between 145 and 158 degrees Fahrenheit. This is the temperature range within which most mashes are conducted. But the temperatures at the high or low ends of this spectrum favor different enzymes. Because of the way the enzymes work, higher mash temps will favor beer with greater body as more unfermentable dextrins will be produced. Mash temps at the lower end of the spectrum will produce a greater amount of fermentable sugars, resulting in beers with a lighter body and slightly higher alcohol content.

When brewing a beer with greater body, some homebrewers will choose to conduct a mash out. A mash out involves raising the temperature of the wort over 170 degrees Fahrenheit. At or above this temperature the enzymes are denatured, and all conversion stops. This will prevent any further enzyme activity and will prevent dextrins from being broken down into fermentable sugars. The added benefit is that by raising the temp of the wort, it makes it easier to drain from the grain bed during the lautering phase.

The amount of water that you are going to use will be dependent upon the amount of grain that you are going to add to the mash. Generally speaking, you will want to add between 1 and 2 quarts of water per pound of grain. If your recipe does not specify an amount, you can split the difference and go with of 1.5 quarts per pound. Obviously there are limits to the amount of grain and water than can fit into one pot. Large grain bills may require you to use less water.

Mashes can be conducted between 145 and 158 degrees Fahrenheit, with most recipes calling for a mash between 150 and 158 degrees Fahrenheit. For reasons discussed in the sidebar (see page 72), the higher the temperature within that range, the less fermentable sugars will be favored and you will have a beer with more body and mouthfeel. The lower the temperature, the less body but the

more fermentable sugars that will be produced, resulting in a slightly higher alcohol content.

The length of the mash—i.e., the amount of time it takes for the enzymes to break the starches down to sugars—is dependent upon the temperature of the mash. A mash conducted at the high end of the spectrum, 158 degrees Fahrenheit, can take as little as 15 minutes, while a mash conducted at 145 degrees Fahrenheit can take up to an hour and half. How do you know when you're done? The easiest option is simply to conduct the mash for an hour. This is usually sufficient, and a good compromise. The other option is to conduct a starch test, which involves taking a small sample of wort and mixing in a drop of iodine. If the wort turns

RIGHT: In order to maintain mash temperatures, some form of insulation is added to otherwise uninsulated mash tuns. In this case, insulation is wrapped around the mash tun for the length of the mash.

blue or black, conversion is not finished; if there is no change in color, you know you are done. When taking your wort sample, you want only a few drops and want to make sure that you do not have any pieces of grain in the sample as it could cause a false positive. It is also easier to do the test on a white plate or tile, as it makes it easier to see the color change.

Lautering

Once you have conducted the mash, the spent grain needs to be separated from the wort. This is called lautering. In homebrewing,

BELOW: This mash tun uses a false bottom to assist in lautering.

PHOTO COURTESY OF RYAN KAHLER

ABOVE: A spigot at the bottom of this mash/lauter tun allows the wort to be drained from the vessel at the end of the mash.

the mash tun traditionally doubles as a lauter tun with a false bottom, manifold, or screen at the bottom of the mash tun. This allows the brewer to separate out the grain as the wort drains from of the vessel.

While the goal is to separate out the wort from the grain, the spent grain is used as a filter material. As the wort flows down and through the grain bed, the bed filters out particulate matter allowing the wort to run clear. Again, this is where the size of the crush comes into play. If the grain was pulverized and the husks were ripped to shreds, the grain will not act as an effective filter bed. Rather the grain will have a flour-like consistency and will clog the filter making it very difficult to remove the wort.

ABOVE: Before the wort has been filtered through the grain bed, it is full of particulate matter.

As discussed in the section on milling, there is a tradeoff between being able to properly set a filter bed and crushing the grain ever finer to increase the amount of sugars that can be extracted from the grain. In order to increase the crush and extract the maximum sugars while setting a proper filter bed, some brewers will add rice hulls to their mash. The rice hulls add filter material to the grain bed without adding fermentable sugars and starches or impacting the flavor of the wort.

When the wort is first allowed to drain from the mash/lauter tun, the first few pints of wort are recirculated back into the mash. The first wort that is drained from the mash will be cloudy until the grain bed starts to act as a filter. Once a proper filter has been established, the wort will run clear and will no longer need to be recirculated back through the grain bed. This is called the vorlauf.

The technique used to drain the wort is dependent upon the method of sparging.

Sparging

Sparging is the process by which the grains are rinsed of excess sugars. When the mash is complete, the wort is sweet and sticky. The sticky wort will cling to the grains but can be rinsed off with hot water. In homebrewing, there are two competing methods of sparging—fly sparging and batch sparging. If you talk to enough homebrewers, you will find that people have very strong opinions about which type of sparging is best. An adherent of one type is likely to be disparaging of the other. The thing to remember is that both methods of sparging will produce excellent beers, and the choice of one over the other is somewhat a matter of personal preference.

Fly Sparging

Fly sparging is the method most often used in commercial breweries and the traditional method used in homebrewing to rinse the grains of excess sugars. Also called continuous sparging, fly sparging requires that the wort be drawn from the grain bed slowly. As the level of the wort drops in the mash tun, hot sparge water (usually 170 degrees Fahrenheit) is replaced on top of the grain bed at an equal rate. The top of the grain bed is not allowed to run dry, and the level of the sparge water is kept just above the top of the grain bed. It is important not to disturb the grain bed, and although not necessary, a sprinkler head is often used to gently replace the wort with sparge water. The sprinkler head is usually gravity fed from a hot liquor tank (HLT). If a sprinkler head is not used, something is usually placed on top of the grain bed to pour the sparge water onto to prevent it from digging into the grain bed and causing channeling.

Fly sparging is the choice of commercial breweries because it allows for greater extract efficiency, and in a properly designed fly sparge system, the homebrewer can achieve greater efficiency as well. Another benefit of fly sparging is that less water is needed than in batch sparging. The amount of sparge water that can be used is dependent upon the amount of water used in the mash. A beer with a very large grain bill will end up using more water in the mash than

a beer with a smaller grain bill. Because of limits to the amount of fluid that any one system can hold, this means that the more wort that is drawn from the mash, the less sparge water that can be added. Unlike batch sparging, which usually requires a volume of sparge water equal to the volume of the water drawn from the mash, fly sparging requires only a small amount of water.

But there are drawbacks to fly sparging. Toward the end of the sparge, the pH of the water leaving the mash tun needs to be monitored. As the sugars are washed from the grain bed, the pH of the runoff will increase. If the pH of the runoff goes above 6, tannins will be extracted from the grain husks, which will add an undesirable astringency to the beer.

Another concern with fly sparging is ensuring that the sparge water is flowing evenly through the grain bed. If the wort and/or sparge water is flowing too quickly it will channel through rather than slowly diffusing through the grain bed. If channeling occurs, only the areas of the grain bed that have sparge water flowing through them will be rinsed clean. Those areas outside of the "channels" will not be properly rinsed, thus lowering your extract efficiency. The manifold placed in the bottom of the MLT is often designed to draw wort from multiple points to avoid issues of channeling.

Another potential concern with fly sparging is drawing the wort off too fast and compacting the grain bed. The grain bed needs to remain loose if the sparge water is going to gently diffuse through it. If the grain bed compacts, the sparge water will no longer flow evenly again resulting in channeling. If the grain bed compacts a lot, you could be faced with a stuck sparge where the wort and sparge water cease to flow out of the MLT.

Batch Sparging

In batch sparging, you allow all of the wort to drain from the MLT before adding any sparge water. After the wort has been fully drained off, the MLT is filled with sparge water and the grain bed is stirred up. After the grain bed has been stirred, the sparge water is fully drained from the mash tun again. This method is not favored by commercial breweries as it is claimed that it results in a lower extract yield than a properly conducted fly sparge. But for the homebrewer the method is simple, and even if the yield is not as good as a fly sparge, this can be compensated for by the addition of a small amount of extra grain. At the scale of a commercial brewery, the extra grain needed to make up for the lost efficiency would be cost prohibitive. But with the standard 5-gallon batch brewed by the homebrewer, the cost is significantly less.

If extract potential were the only concern, the real question would be how much of a difference does fly sparging make over batch sparging. A small-scale experiment run by *Brew Your Own* magazine (Vol 17, No. 3 pages 50–51) involving homebrewing setups showed that it made at most a difference of .004 gravity points and in some cases the choice in sparging method made no difference at all. To put it in starker terms, in the worst case scenario the brewer would have needed to add an extra pound of base grain in a 5-gallon batch, to make up for the "lost" efficiency due to batch sparging. While the experiment run was by no means definitive, it does demonstrate that the extra efficiency from fly sparging is limited.

The design of the MLT in batch sparging is simpler as well. Rather than a manifold that is designed to draw the wort from mul-

PHOTO COURTESY OF RYAN KAHLER

ABOVE: This mash/lauter tun uses a piece of screening to prevent the grain from clogging the drain. Batch sparging works best with an MLT like this.

tiple points at the bottom of the mash tun, the bottom of the mash tun designed for batch sparging can be as simple as a screen to prevent the grain from flowing out with the wort and sparge water. Since the mash tun is going to be completely drained when batch sparging there is less concern about channeling.

There is another alternative to batch and fly sparging: no-sparge. The no-sparge method does exactly as the name suggests and skips the sparge altogether. A very thin mash is used, usually three quarts of water per pound of grain, and the wort is simply drained from the

Brew in a Bag (BIAB)

The Brew in a Bag method is a style of brewing that was developed by homebrewers in Australia. It is essentially a no-sparge method of brewing that prides itself on simplicity. Simply put, the mash is performed by placing the grain in a bag that can be removed from the wort at the end. This is done without a sparge. Because it requires very little in the way of special equipment it is an excellent way for extract brewers to try their hand at all-grain or partial-mash.

Assuming that you already have a large pot (approximately 10 gallons for a 5-gallon brew), the only piece of specialized equipment needed is a large nylon or polyester bag. Most people make their bag out of a fabric called Swiss voile that can be found in a fabric store. It is often used for sheer curtains. The bag needs to be big enough that it can completely line your pot and have plenty of excess up top so that you can grab the bag and lift it out of the pot at the end of the mash.

The grains are crushed very fine and placed in the bag. The mash is going to be very thin, using approximately three quarts of water per pound of grain. Once the water is brought to temp, the bag is placed in the pot and the pot is then covered and insulated. You can insulate the pot by wrapping it in blankets or towels. As with other methods, the mash is performed for about an hour. A mash out can be performed, but is not necessary. After the mash is done, the bag is lifted out and allowed to drain back into the pot. Typically, BIAB is a no-sparge method of brewing. Once most of the wort has drained from the grain, the grains can be given a squeeze to force more wort out.

From this point forward, you follow the standard procedure of bringing the wort to the boil, adding your hop additions, chilling, pitching and fermenting.

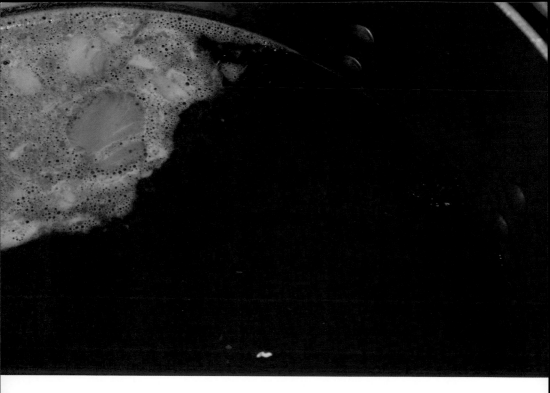

grain bed or, as in the Brew in a Bag method, the grains are lifted out of the wort (see the sidebar). The general consensus is that the no-sparge method results in lower extract efficiencies than either fly sparging or batch sparging. That being said, the method is easily performed without any extra equipment, and for the novice brewer, it can be an easy way to add complexity of taste without adding complexity of process.

The Boil

With extract brews, the only reason for extended boils is to ensure proper hop utilization to achieve proper bittering. There are many other benefits to a full boil, but these have already been realized by the maltster during the production of malt extracts. When brewing with grain, either all-grain or partial-mash, you need to perform the boil yourself.

The boil usually lasts anywhere from one to one and a half hours, and offers a number of benefits to the brewer. The first has to do with hop utilization. The bitter flavor imparted by hops is derived from their alpha acids, and you will usually find this number printed on the package the hops come in. The alpha acids are not directly soluble in water, they first need to be isomerized wherein their molecular structure is changed. While outside of the scope of this book, the isomerization of alpha acids makes them more soluble in water. The amount of isomerization that takes place is a function of time, and the longer the boil, the more bittering compounds that will be dissolved into the wort. This is why bittering hops are added at the beginning of

the boil, to increase the isomerization of the alpha acids found in the hops, whereupon more of them are able to be dissolved into the wort.

Another benefit of the boil is protein coagulation. Conducting a good rolling boil will assist in the coagulation of proteins that will then drop out of the wort. This is the hot break that develops on top of the wort when it first starts to boil. Removing these materials will go a long way toward producing a clean and clear beer. You want to achieve a boil where it appears that the wort is folding over on itself. As the wort boils, protein will clump together and eventually fall out of suspension. This will lead to clearer and hopefully haze-free beer in the end. When the boil first gets going, you need to be mindful of boilovers. This is where a large amount of foam develops on top of the wort due to protein coagulation and spills over the sides of the pot. If you are brewing on a stove top, it is likely to make a sticky mess that is better avoided from the start. Careful attention to the pot as the boil is developing can lessen the risk of a boilover. The wort can be momentarily removed from the heat, or the wort can be stirred to break up the developing foam. This is also a concern with each hop addition.

Another benefit of the boil is that it will cause volatile compounds that form during the brewing process to evaporate out of the wort. Dimethyl sulfide (DMS) is a compound produced in hot wort, which in excessive amounts can give the beer a cooked corn flavor. While certain types of beer can have an acceptable level of DMS, in many styles detectable DMS is considered a flaw. Those types of beer where small amounts of DMS are acceptable are those styles that are traditionally brewed with malts that naturally contain more of the precursors to DMS, especially Pilsner malts. During the boil, DMS will be evaporated out of the wort. As such, the wort should never be covered when it is boiling. Doing so will prevent the evaporation of DMS, leading to unacceptable levels resulting in off-flavors, as the DMS will collect under the lid and run back into the wort.

Finally, a strong rolling boil will assist in the development of flavor and color compounds. Maillard reactions are a browning reaction (the same one that occurs when you toast bread) that is similar to caramelization. (The two are so similar you will hear people incorrectly talking about caramelization occurring during the boil.) The heat of a boil causes Maillard reactions to take place within the wort. Some of the flavors that develop are responsible for the richness of the malt flavor, perceived in some darker beers, without adding body to the beer.

Chilling

Once the boil has been completed, the wort should be chilled as quickly as possible down to the temperature that you want to pitch

the yeast at. This can be done with the use of a wort chiller or using an ice bath. As with the boil, the rapid cooling of the wort will cause further proteins to coagulate and drop out of the wort, increasing the clarity. If these proteins are not dropped out of suspension during the cooling phase, they will coagulate together when the beer is chilled to serving temperatures. This will result in beer that was clear at the time it was bottled but hazy at the time it is served.

Chilling the beer quickly also slows the evaporation of volatile compounds. The flavor and aroma characteristics provided by hops added at the end of the boil would be driven off if they were included at the start of the boil. Chilling the wort stops the evaporation of these volatiles, maintaining both the hop aroma and flavor.

Not only will chilling the beer quickly maintain the hop flavor and aroma, but it will prevent the development of DMS. DMS will only be produced in hot wort, but once you end the boil the existent DMS is no longer being driven off at the same rate. As long as the wort is hot, DMS will continue to build up in the wort. By chilling the wort as quickly as possible you are stopping the formation of DMS and avoiding the off-flavors associated with it.

Finally the wort needs to be brought down to the yeast-pitching temperature. Pitching the yeast at too warm of a temperature can lead to the development of off-flavors. When the yeast is first pitched into the wort it goes through a growth phase before getting to the work of fermentation. During this phase the yeast is producing a number of precursors before alcohol is produced. During a healthy fermentation, the yeast eventually cleans up these precursors. If the temperature is too high when the yeast is pitched, it can accelerate the production of precursors to levels that will not be cleaned up, leaving off-flavors in the beer.

The Process

This process uses a three-vessel brewing system that has been traditionally been used in homebrewing. As discussed in the sidebar on page 83 there are other options such as the Brew in a Bag method, and hybrid approaches can be used. Traditionally, homebrewers have used a system consisting of a boiling vessel, a mash/lauter tun, and a hot liquor tank, the last of which is used to supply hot water to the mash and for sparging. These instructions also presume that you are batch sparging. While both batch sparging and fly sparging can give excellent results, batch sparging is presumed as it is a simpler method for the new all-grain brewer.

Icky Sticky Oatmeal Stout

This stout is named after the mess it left all over the stove the first time it was brewed. There is only a single hop addition, for bittering, as the roasted barley and the oats will take center stage. A very clean yeast should be used—Wyeast 1056 is recommended—to avoid the fruity esters that are the calling card of the Irish yeast that many favor in their stouts.

10 lbs. Marris Otter
2 lbs. Flaked Oats
1.5 lbs. Roasted Barley
0.5 lbs. Chocolate Malt

1 oz. Chinook Hops (added at the start of the boil)

Wyeast 1056 American Ale yeast

Original Gravity Estimate 1.064 (based on 70% efficiency)
Final Gravity Estimate 1.015

IBU 32

1. Yeast

If you are using a liquid yeast and intend to use a starter, you will need to prepare the yeast a few days in advance. Dry yeast can be used without a starter, but it is best to rehydrate the yeast in warm water prior to pitching.

If you are brewing the Oatmeal Stout recipe, make at least a 1-liter starter two days before brew day.

2. Clean and Sanitize

If you are starting to see a trend here, you will notice that cleanliness and sanitization cannot be stressed enough. Your equipment must be kept clean and anything that will come into contact with the wort after the boil will need to be sanitized.

3. Dough-in

The process of actually mixing the grain with the mash water is called "doughing-in." The first step is to bring your mash water to your strike temperature. The strike temperature is the temperature of the water as it is mixed with the grains. The grains will cause the temp of the strike water to drop. Without resorting to calculations, you can estimate that the temperature of the strike water will drop approximately 10 degrees Fahrenheit. The exact amount of the drop will depend on the amount of grains in the mash and their temperature prior to doughing-in.

It is a good idea to preheat your mash tun to avoid further temperature loss. With some systems, the strike water is brought to temp in the mash tun, in which case it is not necessary to specifically preheat the mash tun. If you are using a separate mash tun, such as a converted picnic cooler, it can be preheated by putting approximately a half gallon of boiling water into the mash tun for approximately 10–15 minutes before dough-in (remove the preheating water first).

Whether you add the grain to the water, or the water to the grain, it is very important to thoroughly mix the grain; otherwise dough balls will form. Dough balls will not allow the grain at their center to properly undergo the conversion process, resulting in lower extraction efficiency.

If you miss your targeted mash temperature, the temperature of the mash can be adjusted by adding water to the mash tun. To lower the temperature of the mash, you will add cold water. Conversely, to raise the temperature, you will add hot water. For this reason, it is a good idea to have a second pot of hot water on the stove when you are setting the mash temp. When making changes to the mash temperature, go slowly in order to precisely dial in your target temperature.

With the Oatmeal Stout recipe, bring approximately 4.5 gallons of water to 165 degrees Fahrenheit before mixing in your crushed grain. You want to target a mash temperature of approximately 154 degrees Fahrenheit. Remember to thoroughly mix your grains in to avoid dough balls. Add hot or cold water as needed to reach your target temperature.

4. Mash

Once you have reached your target temperature, the grain will need to steep at the mash temp for approximately one hour to ensure that you have fully converted the starches to sugar. If you are using a converted picnic cooler as a mash tun the mash can simply be covered and left alone. If your mash tun is not insulated, you can wrap the mash tun in a blanket or something similar to add a bit of insulation. It is OK if the temp of the mash drops slightly; you will still achieve conversion.

5. Prepare Your Sparge Water

Toward the end of the mash you will want to prepare your sparge water. The goal in figuring out your water needs is to use enough water during the sparge so that you will reach your target volume at the end of the boil. The first step is to determine how much water you will need. The two key factors in determining the amount of sparge water needed is to account for the water that is absorbed by the grain during the mash and the amount of water that will be lost during the boil.

During the mash, the grain absorbs approximately .1 gallons of water per pound of grain. If you are working with the Oatmeal Stout recipe that has 14 pounds of grain, you can estimate that the grains will absorb approximately 1.4 gallons of water. You can also estimate that you will lose approximately 1 gallon of volume during the boil due to evaporation, which means that you will lose approximately 2.4 gallons of water between the boil and the mash. Since you started with 4.5 gallons of water during dough-in, and your target volume is 5.5 gallons of water, you will need to add another gallon of water to the 2.4 gallons you lose to the grain and evaporation. Accordingly, you will want to sparge with 3.4 gallons of water, which can be safely rounded to 3.5 gallons of water to make things easier.

The sparge water should be heated to between 170 and 180 degrees Fahrenheit.

6. Lauter/Sparge

If you are batch sparging, you will completely drain all wort in the mash tun into the boiling vessel. As discussed, start by removing one or two liters of wort and returning it back to the mash tun; this is the vorlauf. Do this until the wort runs clear of grain particles. Once you have completed the vorlauf, the wort can be drained as quickly as your mash tun will allow. Once the mash tun has completely drained, transfer the hot sparge water to the mash tun and stir the water and grain mixture. Allow it 5–10 minutes to settle and then repeat the vorlauf and completely drain the sparge water into the boiling vessel.

If you are fly sparging, you will need to remove the wort slowly to avoid channeling. After vorlauf, allow the wort to slowly drain until the wort reaches a level just above the grain bed. Gently add an inch or so of sparge water on top of the grain bed. The water can be ladled on top of a plate to avoid disturbing the grain. As the wort is slowly drained from the mash tun, replace the sparge water at the top of the mash tun until you have run out of sparge water and have completely

Fly sparging

drained the mash tun. The entire fly sparging process should take approximately 45 minutes.

7. Boil

After you have finished lautering and sparging, you should have approximately 6.5 gallons of wort in your boil vessel. Bring this to a boil. Be careful as the wort approaches a boil to avoid a boilover. As the hot break develops, you can continuously stir the wort, turn down the heat, or completely remove the pot from heat. It was a lack of paying attention to a boilover that gives the Icky Sticky Oatmeal Stout recipe its name. Once the hot break has subsided, you can return the wort to full heat, hopefully reaching a nice rolling boil.

After you have brought the wort to a boil and gotten past the initial hot break, you can add your bittering hops. If you are making the Oatmeal Stout, you will add all of the hops found in the recipe. If the

recipe you are using calls for the additions of flavor and aroma hops, they will routinely be added when there is 15 minutes left to the boil and at the end of the boil, respectively.

8. Chill

At the completion of the boil, the wort should be chilled as quickly as possible to facilitate the formation of cold break. The wort can be placed in an ice bath, or better yet, a wort chiller can be used to bring the temperature of the wort down to pitching temperatures. You want to use the fastest method that you have available to you, in order to prevent the continuing buildup of DMS and to remove excess proteins.

9. Whirlpool

After the wort has been chilled, it's time to transfer the wort to the fermentation vessel and pitch the yeast. Hot and cold-break material, along with hops and excess grains are still in the wort, and ideally they should be removed. The easiest way to do this is with whirlpooling.

The basic idea is to stir the wort so that wort is moving in a circular fashion. As the wort rotates in the boiling vessel, any particulate matter will move to the center of the vessel where it will settle out in a cone as the wort slows to a stop. After the wort has come to a stop, it can be drained or siphoned from the edges, in such a fashion that the particulate matter that has accumulated in the center is not disturbed and is left behind. While you should strive to keep as much of it out of the fermenter as possible, you need not go to extremes as there is little evidence that the material will affect the final outcome of the beer.

10. Ferment

Once the beer has been transferred to the fermentation vessel it should be vigorously aerated to provide the oxygen that the yeast needs to provide a proper fermentation. If you are using a bucket for

A wine thief can be used to take a sample of the wort for a hydrometer reading.

fermentation, the beer can be passed back and forth from the boiling vessel (after you've dumped the particulate matter from the boiling vessel) to the fermenter a number of times while encouraging splashing. If you are using a carboy, the carboy can be balanced on one edge and pivoted back and forth in order to shake up the wort. Approximately 5 minutes should be sufficient.

The beer should be fermented for at least two weeks, if not longer. A hydrometer reading is the only real way to be sure that fermentation has completed. When the hydrometer reading has leveled off for three days in a row, you can be assured that fermentation is finished and you are ready for bottling or kegging.

⑤
CLEANING AND SANITIZING

BY NOW YOU realize that cleaning and sanitization are of the utmost importance. Every set of instructions (here or elsewhere) starts and ends with the direction to clean your equipment, and proper sanitization is stressed throughout the process. Cleaning and sanitizing are two different aspects of brewing and one cannot be substituted for the other. You cannot sanitize without first cleaning, and cleaning without sanitizing will not suffice either.

Cleaning

In homebrewing, you are aiming for a level of sanitization that will significantly decrease the possibility that your beer will become infected with either wild yeast or bacteria. That level of sanitization cannot be reached if your equipment is dirty. Sanitizers require contact with the microorganism in order to kill it, and if that microorganism is hiding beneath dirt, the sanitizer will never reach it.

It is important to clean your equipment at both the beginning and end of the brewing process. Cleaning your equipment at the end of the session is much easier than if you allow residue and wort to dry onto the equipment and then try to clean it later. Even though you should have cleaned the equipment at the end of the last brew, when you start your next batch it is always best to give the equipment a quick cleaning prior to sanitization.

Mechanical

Cleaning starts with mechanical removal (i.e., scrubbing). Scour pads, such as the Scotch-Brite pad made by 3M, are particularly useful and can be used on both glass and metal. Don't confuse these with the Brillo-type pad, or steel wool. Scour pads are made with plastic and are not likely to scratch your equipment. If you use plastic fermentation and bottling buckets, you need to be extra careful not to use anything that could scratch the plastic. Scratches very hard to fully clean and sanitize, making them an excellent place for bacteria to hide. As plastic buckets are fairly inexpensive, it is better to replace a bucket that has been beat up a little too much rather than chance using it.

It bears repeating, stay away from the steel wool and Brillo. Steel wool will easily scratch plastic equipment, can even scratch glass, and should definitely not be used on stainless steel. Stainless steel is a relatively soft metal, and bits of steel wool can become embedded in it during cleaning. The steel wool will rust and cause the stainless steel to rust as well.

Sodium Percarbonate

Sodium Percarbonates, such as Powdered Brewery Wash (PBW) and OxiClean work extremely well in the homebrewery. OxiClean is readily available and can be found in most grocery stores; you just want to try to obtain the fragrance-free version. PBW is a sodium percarbonate that is perfume-free but contains further additives that make it effective for those with hard water, where OxiClean may not work as well.

One of the great things about sodium percarbonates is that many things can be cleaned simply by soaking them. Once a fermentation vessel has been rinsed out, it can be filled with water and sodium percarbonate and left to sit—it will virtually clean itself. Sodium percarbonates work through oxidation, and as such you need to be careful when using with metals that are prone to oxidation. If left soaking, aluminum can turn black. Stainless steel that is in poor condition could be negatively affected as well. If ever in doubt, do not use percarbonates on your metal pots, but they can be used without fear on all your plastic and glass brewing equipment.

With PBW, follow the manufacturer's instructions. When using OxiClean, use approximately ½ cup to 5 gallons of water. In either case, rinse well after use.

Bar Keepers Friend

Bar Keepers Friend is a general cleaning agent that works particularly well on stainless steel. What makes Bar Keepers Friend well suited to stainless steel is that it will re-passify the steel after use. Passivation is the process that makes stainless steel resistant to oxidation. On stainless steel that has developed some rust spots, not only will the Bar Keepers Friend remove the rust but it will prevent rust from re-forming.

Bar Keepers Friend should not be used on anodized aluminum, but can be used on copper, stainless steel, and glass. It can often be found in the supermarket, but if you can't obtain it there you can order it directly from the manufacturer's website.

Soap

Although not a preferred agent, in a pinch you can use good old-fashioned soap to clean your equipment. Try to use a soap that is free of fragrances and dyes, if at all possible. Make sure to rinse all of the equipment very well, preferably with warm water. You want to make sure that you get all of the soap residue off.

Bleach

Household chlorine bleach can be a good cleaner and an effective sanitizer. But it does have its downsides. Not only can it wreak havoc on your clothes, but it is corrosive to many metals that you are likely to be using in a homebrew setup, including copper and stainless steel. Use at a ratio of one ounce of bleach per gallon of cold water. You want to use a bleach that is free of fragrances, and rinse well as the chlorine can cause off-flavors.

Vinegar

Over time mineral deposits can accumulate on your equipment, especially your boiling vessel. Vinegar is useful in removing mineral deposits from your equipment. Use a ratio of one part vinegar to two parts water. A slightly more diluted mixture of one part vinegar to four parts water can be used if you are going to soak your equipment.

Sanitization

While sanitization is extremely important and not a step to be skipped, it is also not a step to worry about as long as you are taking minimum precautions. You need to always keep in mind that beer was being brewed for hundreds, if not thousands, of years without any understanding of sanitization, or even knowledge of the existence of microorganisms, with great success. While emphasis is placed on sanitization, you need not go to the point of sterilization. Sterilization is the process of eliminating all forms of life, while sanitization is simply the reduction of microorganisms.

There are many ways to sanitize your equipment and ingredients, but our efforts can usually be reduced to two distinct methods—the application of heat and the use of chemical sanitizers.

Heat

Heat is an effective sanitizer, and if taken to the extreme it can be used to sterilize. When you are boiling your wort, you are sanitizing not only the pot your using for the boil, but also the wort itself. This is why special attention should be paid to anything that comes into contact with the wort after the end of the boil, as it will not have the benefit of the sanitizing effects of the boil.

Iodine

Iodine is commonly used for sanitization in homebrewing, usually as Iodophor, a preparation containing iodine complexed with a solubilizing agent, but there are a number of other preparations available. Iodophor needs a contact time of 5 minutes and if used at the proper ratios does not need to be rinsed. Do *not* use it straight from the bottle—it needs to be diluted with water. Follow the manufacturer's instructions as different manufacturers prepare the solution at different concentrations. Note that it will stain plastic. Unlike acid-based sanitizers such as Star San, Iodophor cannot be stored once it has been diluted.

Acid-Based

Acid-based sanitizers, such as Star San from Five Star Chemicals (the same company that makes PBW), are another very popular choice. Star San has two big advantages over Iodophor, the first is that unused sanitizer can be stored (nearly indefinitely if you use distilled water to dilute it) without losing its effectiveness and, second, it has a shorter minimum contact time of one minute. Like Iodophor, Star San is a no-rinse sanitizer.

No need to fear the foam; it is perfectly safe and won't ruin your beer.

Since diluted Star San retains its effectiveness for a long period of time, you can keep a preparation of Star San in a spray bottle. This becomes extremely useful when you need to quickly sanitize items such as the mouth of a carboy when racking to a bottling bucket or the outside of a yeast packet before pitching into a starter.

Star San also has a tendency to foam up when being prepared. The foam itself acts as a sanitizer and is useful in making sure that you are sanitizing those hard to reach places and ensuring contact time. As Star San is a no-rinse sanitizer, you need not worry about the foam and you can safely transfer wort or fermented beer into the foam without it having any effect on final product.

Bleach

As indicated above, household bleach can be a good cleaner and an effective sanitizer. Use at a ratio of one ounce of bleach per gallon of cold water. Do not use warm water, as it will cause the chlorine to evaporate out of the solution and remove its ability to sanitize. It requires a contact time of 10 minutes and you will need to rinse the equipment after it has been sanitized. If you use bleach, always use one that is free of fragrances.

Removing Labels from Bottles

Removing labels from commercial bottles prior to bottling is a subject that always seems to garner a lot of attention. This is probably because no one method seems to be foolproof. Most methods rely on soaking the bottles in some sort of solution.

A common, and perhaps the easiest and most effective, method is to soak the bottles in OxiClean or PBW overnight. Most labels will float right off, and you have the added benefit that they will be clean when you are done, requiring at most a good rinsing. Other popular methods of removing labels include soaking in a water and vinegar solution or soaking in a preparation of Star San.

PART II

Ingredients

crafts, the quality of your product will be directly attributable in part to the quality of your materials. Start with inferior ingredients and you will never produce an exceptional beer. Marry fresh ingredients with technique and the end result has a better chance of ending up as something special.

The primary ingredients in beer are water, malted barley, hops, and yeast. You may be familiar with the German Reinheitsgebot (often referred to as the German Beer Purity Law), which famously holds that beer shall be brewed using those four ingredients and no others. In fact, when the Reinheitsgebot was originally drafted it didn't even allow for yeast, as its role in brewing had yet to be discovered. Although commonly referred to as the "German" beer law, it was originally limited to the state of Bavaria. Outside of Bavaria, it was not observed although various regions may have had their own laws governing brewing. An example of a beer that does not conform to the law is the Hefeweizen, which is brewed with a large proportion of wheat— not one of the four permissible ingredients under the Reinheitsgebot.

The original purpose of the law is debatable; some commentators have speculated that it was the first food purity law and that it was designed to prevent unscrupulous brewers from adding less than quality fermentables as substitutes for barley. Other commentators have speculated that the law was a sort of rationing, designed to prevent brewers from buying up other grains that were used by professions such as bakers, thus keeping price of bread under control. Although the law is no longer in effect in any legally binding fashion, many German brewers adhere to the spirit of the law as a testament to their commitment to using only the finest ingredients.

While wheat is a common alternative fermentable found in beer today, it is far from the only one—rye is often used for its spicy character and rice is famously used in American-Style Lagers. In addition to rice, direct sugar injections are not unheard of in order to provide more fermentables or as a way to provide unfermentable sugars that will contribute to body and mouthfeel.

Fermentables are not the only place where adjunct ingredients are found. The use of fruit is quite common, and classic examples can be found in Belgian Lambics. All manner of spices are used as well, and are almost a requirement in the Winter Warmers that are gaining popularity during the winter holiday season. While commercial examples can be found for each of these additions, the commercial brewers have nothing on innovative homebrewers who are limited only by their imagination.

THE PRIMARY INGREDIENT in beer is water, but too often the homebrewer fails to give it any attention. The amount of attention that your water source will require will depend upon the type of brewing that you are going to do. An extract brewer need only take some simple precautions, while any brewer undertaking a mash will need to give their water a little more thought.

For the extract brewer, most potable water will do as long as it smells and tastes acceptable. If your water has a strong chlorine smell, it may be treated with chloramine, which is used by municipalities to kill bacteria. Unlike chlorine, which can be boiled off, chloramine is more stable and will require treatment. The most common way to deal with chloramine is to use a Campden tablet, which can be obtained at most homebrew stores. Campden tablets contain sodium

6
WATER

metabisulphite, and if you are preparing all of you are water ahead of time, one tablet will be sufficient to eliminate both chlorine and chloramine from your water.

With all-grain brewing, water treatment can become more complicated. At the very least you should ask your local water authority for a copy of the area water report, which will give you a breakdown of the minerals found in your water. Without going into too much detail, at the very least you want to make sure that your water has at least 50ppm of calcium. If your water is very soft and does not have 50ppm of calcium, you can adjust your water by adding 1 teaspoon of gypsum per 5 gallons of water. There are hundreds of adjustments that you can make to your brewing water, but tweaking water chemistry is really only necessary in very advanced brewing and is beyond the scope of this book.

MALTS per

Crystal/color:
Briess Crystals - $2
Carahell - $2.25
CaraPib - $2
CaraMunich I + III - $2.50
Caravienne - $2
Dark Crystal - $2
CaraRed - $2
Honey Malt - $2.25
Special B - $2.50
CaraMunch - $2.50
Biscuit - $2.25
Aromatic - $2.25
Brown - $2.50
Victory - $2.25
Vienna - $2
Special Roast - $2.25

MALTS:
Chocolate - $2.25
Pale Chocolate - $2.25
Chocolate Rye - $2.50
Black Patent - $2.50
Carafa spec. II - $2
Roasted Barley - $2.25
Munich 10L + 20L - $2.25
Amber - $2.25

Adjuncts
Flaked Barley $1.50
Flaked Wheat $1.50
Flaked Rye $2
Flaked Oats $2
Rice Hulls $1.50

Base
Rahr 2-Row - $1.50
Rahr 6-Row - $1.50
Wheat Malt - $1.50
Maris Otter - $2
German Pils - $2
Rye Malt - $2
Belgian Pils - $2
Acidulated - $2.50
Peat Smoked - $2.50
Beech Smoked - $2.50
Golden Oats - $2.25
Valley Malt $2.25
Pale, NE Grown
Organic

A large assortment of malts are available to the homebrewer.

⑦
MALTS

BARLEY IS MALTED in the three-step process consisting of steeping, germination, and drying. The barley is first steeped in water for up to 48 hours. During this time, the moisture content of the grain increases from approximately 12 percent to 44 percent. The uptake of water activates enzymes that cause the barley to germinate, and causes new enzymes to develop that will make the starches in the grain available for later use by the brewer during the mash. During steeping, the barley is occasionally roused and exposed to air to ensure that the grain is obtaining enough oxygen.

During steeping, the maltster carefully observes the barley and removes it from the water just as the endosperm, or the plant shoot, is starting to show. The barley is then removed from the water and is allowed to germinate. The grain is often spread on the floor of a large room, where humid air is passed through the grain as it is turned. This maintains the moisture content of the grain and prevents the growing endosperms from matting together. In unmalted barley the enzymes necessary to convert starch into fermentable sugar are present but in a form that cannot be used during the mash. Germination releases these enzymes, making them available during the mashing process. The amount of enzymes present is the grain's diastatic power—its ability to convert starch to sugar—and is measured in degrees Lintner.

ABOVE: A steeping vessel.

BELOW: The giant screws seen in this picture are used to turn the grain
while it germinates.

ABOVE: A close up of germinated rye; the endosperm can be clearly seen.

The degree to which the malt is allowed to germinate determines the level of the grain's "modification," although modification is not the same as diastatic power. Modification is the extent to which the starches found in the grain are made soluble so that they are available to the enzymes in the mash. Highly modified malts also have less complex proteins, which can cause haze in the finished product. The further along the maltster allows the grain to germinate, the longer the sprout grows, and the more modified the malt becomes. The problem is that the more the grain is allowed to sprout, the more it uses up the starches as the endosperm grows. This is the art of the maltster, knowing when to stop germination, balancing modification with available starch.

Highly modified malts also have amino acids that are available as yeast nutrients to aid in fermentation. Historically, malts were undermodified and didn't have the amino acids necessary for a healthy fermentation. In order to address this problem the brewer would perform a protein rest by steeping the grains at approximately

ABOVE: A modern grain kiln.

125 degrees Fahrenheit for 20 minutes. A protein rest was used to encourage proteolytic conversions, wherein proteins are broken down into the amino acids needed as yeast nutrients. Today, most malts available to the homebrewer are highly modified, and, as such, a protein rest is not necessary.

Once the malt has germinated, it is then dried in a kiln. Often, kilning takes place in the same room as germination. Instead of humid air, hot, dry air is now passed through the grain, which stops the germination process and dries out the malt to about 4 percent moisture content. Many of the characteristic colors and flavors of the malt are developed during kilning.

The color of the grains, and the color they impart to the beer, is measured in degrees lovibond. Low lovibond ratings, such as those found in base malts, will impart a straw color to the beer. As the lovibond rating increases, the colors pass through oranges, reds, and browns on their way to black.

ABOVE: An early twentieth-century kiln. Hot air would be circulated up from under the floor, and the shovels in the far corner would be used to turn the grain by hand.

Base Grains

Base grains are the backbone of a beer, and are often labeled as "Brewers Malts." They provide the greatest amount of fermentables and the enzymes necessary to convert starch to sugar. Most base grains have great enough diastatic power to not only convert their own starches, but also to convert the starches of other grains with low diastatic power. Those grains that contain enough enzymes to convert their own starches to sugar are called self-converting. Many types of specialty malts are not self-converting and therefore must be mashed with grains that contain more enzymes than necessary to

convert their own starches. Base grains are kilned but not roasted, and thus usually have very low lovibond ratings.

2-Row and 6-Row

Generally brewers use two varieties of barley: 2-row and 6-row. The designation refers to the number of rows of kernels that are formed on the plant. The kernels on 2-row barley are plumper and contain less husk material than the 6-row variety, and 2-row is generally considered to have more of a malty taste as opposed to a grain-like flavor associated with 6-row. The 6-row variety generally has more diastatic power than the 2-row variant. Although 2-row varieties are used more often, the higher diastatic power of 6-row is sometimes favored when brewing with a large amount of adjunct grains such as corn or rice that are low in, or have no, enzymes. The extra husk material of 6-row is sometimes a benefit when brewing with grains that are known to cause sparging problems, such as wheat or oats. Both 2-row and 6-row malt usually have a lovibond rating coming in around 1–2.

Maris Otter

Maris otter is a slightly darker variant of 2-row barley. Often used in English ales, where it provides a rich malt character. Maris

Otter has a lovibond rating around 2–4. Other traditional British base malts include Optic and Pearl.

Pale Malt

Pale Malt usually has a lovibond rating between 2 and 4. Used over basic 2-row or 6-row to give a slightly darker color and more of a biscuit-like flavor.

Golden Promise

A variant of barley that is native to Scotland. Usually has a lovibond rating around 3 and provides a rich malt backdrop for Scottish and British Ales.

Pilsner Malt

A variant of malted barley that provides a very pale color with a lovibond rating usually below 2, it is very low in protein, which helps achieve a very clear finished product. Traditionally used in German and Czech (Bohemian) pilsners. Region-specific varieties can often be found for a touch of authenticity.

Malts That Can Be Steeped

Not all malts can be steeped; many require a mash in order to contribute to the final character of the beer. The following types of malt can be steeped to contribute flavor and color to the beer, but they will not contribute any fermentables unless they have been mashed.

Kilned Malts

These are malts that are kilned at a higher temperature, or for longer, than base malts. Kilned malts usually have enough enzymes to self-convert, but not enough to convert adjunct grains. They can be mashed, or small amounts can be steeped in order to impart flavor and color to the wort without fermentables.

Munich Malt

A pale malt found as the primary malt in Oktoberfest and Vienna lagers, it is kilned at a higher temperature than basic pale malt, and is sometime referred to as being toasted. With a lovibond rating up to 10, it provides a dark red color and a malty sweetness, though not to the extent of crystal malts. While Munich malt contains enough enzymes to convert its own starches, it does not have enough enzymes to convert starches from adjuncts.

Vienna Malt

Like Munich malt, it is toasted or kilned at a higher temperature although not to the same degree. It has a lovibond rating up to 4 and is the primary contributor to the flavor profile of a Vienna lager. Vienna malt is able to self-convert.

Smoked Malts

Smoked Malt

Smoked malt is usually a pale malt base grain that has been smoked over wood chips to add a smoked flavor. While the grain contains enzymes and can be mashed, it can be steeped when using it in an extract brew to contribute color and flavor but won't contribute any fermentables to the wort. Each malt house has their specific style of smoked malt, and smoked malts can be found that have been smoked over cherry or beech wood. Additionally, the homebrewer also has the option of smoking his or her own malt. Lovibond ratings are usually low, between 2 and 5. Smoked malts give German Rauchbiers their characteristic smoky flavor but can also be used in porters and stouts.

Peated Malt

A type of smoked malt that has been smoked over peat. Used in Scottish ales, it usually has a much stronger flavor than a standard smoked malt. As with other smoked malts, the lovibond rating is low, usually less than 5.

Crystal or Caramel Malts

Crystal malts are often used to increase head retention, body, and mouthfeel, by adding unfermentable sugars to the wort. They can be used anywhere up to 15 percent of the grain bill. Crystal malts are the only malted grain that can add sugars to the beer without needing to undergo a mash, as the sugars are developed during the kilning process. As with other malts, crystal malts are allowed to germinate. Instead of being transferred immediately to dry heat, the green malt (malt that has not been kilned) is "stewed" in a very damp oven. This creates a mini-mash that causes the starches to convert to sugars, which are locked into the grain when it is cooled. After the grain has been stewed, it is then transferred to a dry kiln. It is during its time in the dry kiln that the malt takes on its color and flavor characteristics as the sugars undergo caramelization.

BELOW: Crystal malts come in a number of different lovibond ratings. 10 L is on the left, while 120 L is on the right.

Crystal Malts are sold in a range of styles that are designated by their color profile, usually spanning a range between 10 and 120 degrees lovibond. As the lovibond rating increases, the malt will contribute a darker color to the wort ranging from light straw (10 L) through deep reds (120 L). In addition to color, the flavor and aroma profile will change as well, with increased caramel flavors and aromas becoming dominant as the lovibond rating increases.

One thing to be aware of is that each maltster has their own method for making crystal malts, and as such, there is no consistency between malt houses. Flavor characteristics as well as color can change for two products bearing similar lovibond ratings. Furthermore, many malt houses make other types of crystal malts, by changing the base grain or using malts that have been kilned longer or at a higher temperature. These are sold under names like Dextrin, Carapils, Special B, and Extra Dark Crystal.

Roasted Malts

Roasted malts are heated twice by the maltster. As with all malts, the grain is first dried in a kiln. The length of time that the grain spends in the kiln along with the temperature of the air that is blown through the grain can be increased to start browning reactions. Roasted malts are taken a step further and transferred to a roaster after kilning, where they pick up further color and depth of flavor. The roaster usually consists of a large drum that is slowly turned, ensuring that the grains are evenly roasted to guarantee consistent results.

BELOW: A variety of caramel malts are available to the homebrewer.

PHOTO COURTESY OF WEYERMANN SPECIALTY MALTS

ABOVE: Roasting drums

The temperatures involved in the production of roasted malts have been shown to produce antioxidants, which aid in an increased shelf life of the beer. For this reason, beers that are designed for long-term storage usually contain some of the darker specialty grains.

Black Patent/Black Malt

Black Patent is so named because the method for making it was patented when it was first developed. With a lovibond ranging from 500 to 700, a small amount of Black Patent will contribute a very dark color to the wort without affecting the head of the beer. In small quantities it contributes little flavor, but in larger quantities it can contribute an acrid bitterness to the beer. It is often used in porters.

Roasted Barley

Roasted barley is one of the only specialty grains that is not malted—the raw grain is sent straight to the roasting drum. The

LEFT: Black patent

roasted barley gives the finished beer a dry-roasted coffee flavor that is sought after in stouts. It can also be found in porters, but some will argue that the defining characteristic that separates stouts from porters is the use of roasted barley. Lovibond values can range from 300 to 650, although at the higher end some maltsters label it as Black Barley.

Victory

With a lovibond rating of about 20, victory malt will impart a dry-toasted malt flavor that works well in English ales.

Biscuit

Used to give a toasted flavor to ales, with a lovibond rating of up to 20. Imparts an amber to mahogany color to the beer depending on the amount used. Biscuit does not have enough enzymes to self-convert.

RIGHT: Roasted barley

Other Malts and Adjuncts

Barley is not the only type of grain that is malted for brewing purposes. Many styles of beer require the addition of, or are made almost entirely from, other types of grains including wheat and rye. Other styles of beer require the addition of adjuncts, such as rice or corn.

Wheat

After barley, wheat is the most commonly used malted grain in brewing. Weissbeirs and Witbiers are made primarily from wheat. Due to wheat's high protein content, wheat beers are usually hazy.

BELOW: Wheat

Rye

Wheat is usually ground finer than barley, and it does not have a husk. As such, beers brewed with a large amount of wheat often have trouble during lautering and sparging. Wheat malt usually has a color of less than 3 L, although it does seem to impart less color to the wort than its lovibond rating would suggest. Wheat has very high levels of beta-glucans, which can cause the mash to gum up. In order to avoid this problem a beta-glucan rest is often performed by holding the temp of the mash at about 100 degrees Fahrenheit for 20 minutes before bringing the temperature of the mash up to conversion temps.

Rye

Like wheat, rye does not have a husk. It is noted for the spicy character it can impart to the beer. Rye can have a lovibond rating between 2 and 4. As with wheat, rye is very high in beta-glucans, which can create a sticky mash and may necessitate a beta-glucan rest if used as a high proportion of the grain bill.

Oats

Oats are used to impart a creamy mouthfeel to the beer. Although they aid body, they can have a negative impact on head retention due to oils in the grain. Traditionally used in Belgian witbeers and some stouts, a high protein content can add to haze in the finished product.

Corn

Although the use of corn has been derided as a cost-saving measure of the large brewers that produce American-Style Lager, corn does have its place in brewing. It provides an extremely fermentable source of sugar that is very low in proteins, which allows for the production of a crystal clear, dry beer. It can also be used in darker-style beers to add alcohol content without increasing body.

Rice

Like corn, rice adds fermentable sugars with a low amount of protein that allows for the production of dry, crystal clear beer.

Hop cone in the Yakima Valley.

⑧
HOPS

HOPS PROVIDE BITTERING, flavor, and aroma to the beer and generally contribute to the overall character of the beer including mouthfeel, perception of bitterness, and fullness. The importance of hops in beer cannot be overestimated. While some styles of beer such as India Pale Ales are known for their hop profiles, hops is important in balancing out the malt profile even in beers that are not known for their hops. While beers can certainly be brewed without hops—generally using other flavoring additives in its place—for many beer lovers, a beer without hops is not really beer at all.

Hops are harvested from the vine of the plant named *Humulus lupulus*, which is related to cannabis and catnip. Only the female plant produces the hop cones used in brewing. Hop vines (properly called "bines") can grow up to twenty-feet tall and are usually supported by strings. When the hops are ready to harvest, the entire bine is cut down and the cones are removed. The hop cones are then taken to an "oast house" or hop kiln where the cones are dried out by passing hot air through them. Certain regions are known for their hop production, such as the Willamette and Yakima Valleys in the Northwest United States, and local hops are often a part of the character of the regional beer styles. The bitter grapefruit flavor of the hops grown in Northwest United States are able to offset the large malt profiles of

American-Style IPA, while the spicy flavor and flowery aroma derived from Sazz hops complements the light-style Bohemian pilsner.

Aside from aiding in flavor and aroma, hops have numerous other benefits as well. Hops have well-known antibacterial properties, providing a measure of protection from potentially beer-spoiling microorganisms. Furthermore, hops have been shown to aid in flavor stability and head retention, and, as a last resort, hop aroma has been shown to at least mask beer staling.

Beer bitterness and hoppy aroma are due to alpha-acid and essential oils found in the lupulin glands. If you were to look at a cross section of a hop flower you would see the stem, which is called a "strig." Coming off of the strig are the "bracts," which is just a fancy name for the specialized leaves found in the hop flower. The "bracteole" are the smaller leaves, at the base of which you find the lupulin glands. Depending on the type of hop, the lupulin can vary in quantity and

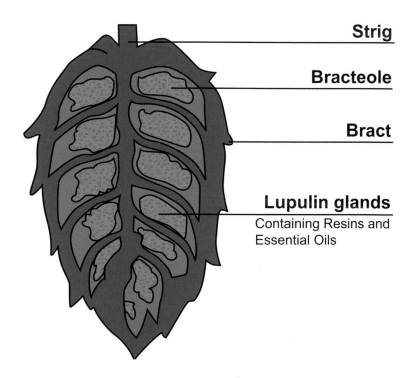

Strig

Bracteole

Bract

Lupulin glands
Containing Resins and
Essential Oils

can be pale yellow to golden color. Generally speaking, the more bitter the hop, the greater the quantity of lupulin.

Bitterness is primarily attributable to the alpha acids found in the lupulin gland. Alpha acids are not soluble in water, and thus need to be converted to iso-alpha acids, which *are* soluble in water. This is accomplished by boiling the hops for an extended period of time. The longer the boil, the more alpha acids will be converted to iso-alpha acids and be dissolved into the wort. The more iso-alpha acids, the more bitter the beer will be.

The problem is that the boiling process causes volatile essential oils from the hops to be lost to evaporation. Primarily this affects the aroma and flavor compounds, but to a certain extent even those compounds associated with bittering. Although it can take up to an hour to extract the bittering compounds from the hops, by the end of the boil most, if not all, of the aroma and flavor of the hops have been lost. Therefore, further hop additions are required toward the end of the boil. Flavor additions are usually made with less than 30 minutes left on the boil, while aroma additions are normally made with less than 5 minutes left on the boil or even when the wort is taken off of the heat.

While bittering components derived from hops have been shown to be relatively stable once the boil is over, other components contributing to aroma and to a lesser extent flavor are more prone to degradation over an extended storage time. Despite this, at least one study has shown that the addition of late hops, either at the end of the boil or during whirlpooling, has at the very least masked beer staling.

Hops are available to the homebrewer in many forms. The most common form for hops to be sold in is a pellet. Hop pellets are made by chopping up the whole leaf hop cones and pressing them into pellets. There are several advantages to hop pellets. First, pellets are the most stable form for storage. Because of the relatively low surface area of the pellet, less oxidation occurs. Also related to storage, hop pellets take up the least amount of storage space. Finally, hop pellets offer greater alpha-acid utilization, requiring less hops to obtain the same amount of bitterness. There are some drawbacks to pellet hops,

ABOVE: Hop pellets

BELOW: Hop plugs

ABOVE: Whole leaf hops

as the process used to create the pellet drives off some of the aroma
and flavor potential.

Hops are also available whole leaf and as plugs. Whole leaf hops
are simply the dried out hop cones while hop plugs are whole leaf hop
cones that have been pressed into a disk resembling a small hockey
puck. While whole leaf hops may have greater flavor and aroma characteristics, they have a tendency to degrade
over time once exposed to air. Hop plugs are
somewhat less prone to degradation as they
have less surface area exposed to air. When
using whole leaf hops, it is best to use them
quickly to avoid degradation in quality.

No matter what form of hops you purchase,
you want to make sure that you get the freshest
available. When you purchase the hops from

RIGHT: When purchasing hops, make
sure that they are fresh. They should be
vacuum-sealed and refrigerated.

· · 137 · ·

Hops growing in the
Yakima Valley.

your local homebrew store make sure that they are being stored in a refrigerator, which helps preserve them while in storage. Additionally, hops are often available in either a vacuum-sealed bag or a bag that has been flushed with nitrogen, both of which will help preserve the flavor and aroma.

There are a number of ways that hops are used. Each use brings out different characteristics of the hops, and, often, multiple methods will be employed in the same beer.

Boiling

In order to obtain the bitter character of hops, the hops need to be boiled. As discussed, the bittering capability of hops are directly related to the amount of alpha acids available, and boiling causes a chemical change to occur wherein the alpha acids, which are not soluble in water, become iso-alapha acids, which are. The degree to which this occurs is dependent on time and temperature. As the boiling process tends to drive off the more volatile oils associated with flavor and aroma, boiling time for those hop additions is usually limited.

It is useful to be able to estimate the bitterness of your beer. The amount of alpha acids in any one type of hop can vary from year to year and crop to crop. By being able to calculate the bitterness levels of the beer, you can make adjustments based upon the hops you have on hand. This will also let you make adjustments if you need to substitute one type of hop for another due to a lack of availability. (It is not necessary to learn to calculate bitterness levels, and many people make wonderful beer without ever thinking of these things, but if you want to know, read on.)

There are a number of ways to quantify the bitterness of a beer. Traditionally, homebrewers used a measurement called the Homebrew Bitterness Unit or HBU. While this method is no longer widely used, you may come across old recipes that use this formulation. Sometimes you will find HBUs listed as Alpha Acid Units or AAUs. HBUs can be calculated by multiplying the amount of hops measured in ounces by the alpha-acid percentage. If you were to use 2 ounces of a bittering hop with an alpha acid percentage of 11 percent, the final product would have 22 HBU.

HBUs give you a very rough idea of the bitterness level, and more precise ways to estimate the bitterness of beer have been established. The preferred method of calculating the bitterness derived from hops is to estimate the amount of alpha acids that actually make it into the beer, and this is measured in International Bitterness Units, routinely referred to as IBU. This is the measurement that is often found on the labels of commercial beers trying to out compete one another in how "hoppy" they can make their beers.

The difference between HBUs and IBUs is that IBUs attempt to determine the amount of the alpha acids that actually make it into the beer. Quite a few authors have run experiments in order to determine hop utilization, but unfortunately they have not reached a consensus. Dr. Michael Hall in an article in *Zymurgy* (the magazine of the American Homebrewers Association), after reviewing much of the available literature of the time, recommends the following two equations. The IBU estimate for you beer is determined by adding the two values together.

For bittering hops, added at the start of the boil, use this equation:

$$IBU = \frac{(18.7 \times \text{Weight in Ounces} \times \text{Alpha Acid}\%)}{\text{Gallons of Beer}}$$

For hops that are to be used as a flavor addition, and boiled for less than 30 minutes, use this equation:

$$IBU = \frac{(7.5 \times \text{Weight in Ounces} \times \text{Alpha Acid}\%)}{\text{Gallons of Beer}}$$

The only difference between the two is the constant (18.7 in the first equation and 7.5 in the second equation) that accounts for the change in utilization that occurs based upon the length of time that the hops are being boiled. As flavor hops are boiled for a shorter length of time than the bittering hop addition, far less of the alpha acids are being used.

Late Hops

Aroma hops are added at the very end of the boil, with either just a few minutes left to the boil or at flame out. The essential oils that contribute to aroma are very volatile and are driven off by boiling. As aroma hops are not boiled for very long, if at all, they do not contribute to the bitterness of the beer at all and their contribution to either HBUs or IBUs is considered zero.

Dry Hopping

Dry hopping is a technique wherein hops are added to the beer after fermentation, during the conditioning phase. The hops are allowed to soak in the beer for anywhere from three days to two weeks. This allows the essential oils to seep into the beer, without being driven off by heat from hot wort. Dry hopping is usually performed with whole leaf or plug hops, but pellets can be used.

Dry hopping contributes to the aroma and flavor of the beer, but does not contribute to bitterness in any meaningful way. It is a good idea to sample the beer while dry hopping, and remove the hops when the desired flavor is reached as extended dry hopping can lead to a grassy flavor in the beer which can become undesirable if it becomes too pungent.

First Wort Hops

First wort hops is a method that is used in all-grain brewing. Instead of waiting to add the hops at the start of the boil, the hops are added to the boiling vessel when the wort is drained into the kettle

Whole leaf hops are preferred for dry hopping. Plugs will also work well.

from the MLT. While flavor and aroma compounds tend to be driven off during the boil, it is believed that chemical changes take place that make these compounds less volatile and prone to evaporation during boiling. As such, first wort hops can impact flavor and aroma despite the long boil time.

Hop Back

Another method of using hops, utilizes a device called a hopback. A hopback is a container that holds the hops while the hot wort is passed through it. The hops act as a filter, clarifying the wort as it passes through the hopback on its way to a chiller. The hopback is fully enclosed so the volatile oils that contribute flavor and aroma do not evaporate out of the wort.

YEAST ARE SINGLE cell organisms, and for such small creatures, yeast have a big impact on your beer. They affect not only the body and feel of the beer, but they make a large contribution to flavor and aroma. Fermentation converts sugars in the wort into alcohol, drying the beer out while the specific gravity drops. But alcohol is not the only product of fermentation—a number of other by-products are produced, including esters, fusel alcohols, and diacetyl, among others

9

YEAST

that can contribute both wanted and unwanted flavors and aromas. In fact, it has been estimated that yeast can contribute up to five hundred different flavor compounds to a beer.

Brewers divide yeast into two groups, lager yeasts and ale yeasts. As their names suggest, lager yeasts are used to make lagers while ale yeasts are used to produce ales. Generally speaking, ale yeasts are described as being top fermenting as the cells are highly floccu-

ABOVE: When purchasing yeast you want to buy fresh samples that have been properly stored.

lant, which means that they readily clump together. As the yeast cells clump together they capture some of the carbon dioxide that is being produced and rise to the top of the fermentation vessel. There they form a thick "krausen" (a foamy head that develops on top of the wort during the initial stage of fermentation) and are easily harvested from the fermentation vessel for future use. Lager yeast cells, on the other hand, tend to stay in suspension longer and ultimately settle out of the beer at the bottom of the fermenter. This distinction has become somewhat blurred as the number of strains of yeast has multiplied in recent years, and it is possible to find ale yeasts that don't flocculate very well and lager yeasts that do.

The primary purpose of the yeast is to convert sugars to alcohol, but it doesn't go about this in a direct fashion. After you have pitched the yeast it goes through four phases as it travels along the journey that will convert sugar to alcohol: the lag, growth, active fermentation, and flocculation/settling. Although we will discuss fermentation being in one phase or another, it is important to real-

ize that to some extent all four phases are happening simultaneously. When we discuss each phase, we are speaking about what the
yeast is doing generally as a population, rather than what any one
yeast cell is up to.

Immediately after pitching, the yeast enters what is referred to
as the lag phase. This is the period wherein very little obvious activity
is taking place. Although you can't see it, the yeast is preparing for
growth and fermentation by taking up nutrients and oxygen. Most of
the nutrients needed by the yeast are found in the malt except for the
necessary oxygen, thus the need for adequate aeration at the time of
pitching. In an all-malt beer, or a beer made with little adjuncts, there
is adequate nutrition for the yeast. In most cases oxygen is the limiting factor. Without the necessary oxygen, yeast growth is restricted,
which can result in flavor changes in the beer.

After the yeast has taken up the necessary nutrients and oxygen,
it goes through the growth phase. The size of individual yeast cells
does not significantly change; rather when we say growth, we are
talking about the population of yeast in the wort. Yeast reproduces
by budding, wherein a "daughter cell" starts to grow or bud from the
side of the parent cell, until it breaks free. During the growth phase,
the number of yeast cells will grow at an exponential rate until the
necessary nutrients become scarce, slowing further growth. During
the lag and growth phase the yeast is not only taking up nutrients, but
is also producing a number of by-products These by-products will
have a huge impact on the flavor of the beer.

By the time the growth has slowed, the yeast has entered the
active fermentation stage. During active fermentation the yeast is
converting sugars to alcohol. Yeast will start by converting the simplest sugars first, such as fructose and glucose, before moving onto
the longer chain sugars such as maltose and maltotriose. The yeast
does not convert sugars directly to alcohol; rather, there are intermediary steps that produce some additional flavor compounds. Furthermore, the production of alcohol allows additional reactions to
take place, such as the synthesis of esters, which are formed by condensing fatty acids created during yeast growth with alcohols. Esters

To Secondary or Not to Secondary?

Within homebrewing there a number of methods that cause lively debate; one of these methods is whether to "secondary" or not. The process of using a secondary fermentation involves racking (transferring) the beer—once active fermentation has stopped or when it has significantly slowed—to another fermenter in order to remove the beer from the yeast that has accumulated on the bottom of the fermenter. Originally, it was believed that if the beer was left for too long on top of the yeast cake autolysis would occur, wherein the yeast cells rupture and leak their insides into your beer with some resulting nasty off-flavors.

There is some debate as to whether autolysis really occurs under homebrew conditions, which are significantly different than commercial brewery conditions where autolysis can be a real problem. There is some speculation that autolysis may have been more of a problem in the early days of homebrewing when high-quality yeasts were not available. Autolysis may also be a problem when the beer is stored on top of the yeast cake for an exceptionally significant period—a period that would most certainly be measured in months, not weeks.

Even without the specter of autolysis, there are still some who argue that a secondary is a beneficial aid to obtaining clear beer, since every time you rack the beer from one container to the next you tend to pull some yeast back into suspension. Although there is some truth to this, the benefits of leaving the beer on the yeast cake far outweigh any beneficial clarifying effect. As long as the beer remains in contact with the yeast, the yeast are continuing to have an effect on the beer. Any number of precursors and by-products are cleaned up, including diacetyl and acetaldehyde, as maturation occurs.

are a significant contributor to beer flavor and are often associated with fruit- and floral-like tastes.

Once active fermentation has ceased or slowed, the yeast enters the flocculation/settling phase. During this phase the yeast starts to settle out of the beer. The more flocculant the yeast strain, the quicker this will occur. Ale yeast can sometimes settle out in a few days while lager yeast can sometimes take weeks to fully clear. Although the yeast has converted the majority of sugars by this point, it will continue to work on some of the by-products, including diacetyl, breaking them down further into tasteless compounds.

The process of breaking down by-products and converting precursors continues as long as the beer is allowed to mature, and all beers will benefit from maturation. The off-flavors associated with diacetyl and acetaldehyde are some of the flavors associated with "young" or "green" beer. These flavors subside and/or disappear altogether with proper aging with the beer still in contact with the yeast.

At this point lagers are traditionally aged in cold storage—a process known as lagering. Because lager yeasts work at colder temperatures than ale yeasts, the process of maturation takes significantly longer, and because the yeast do not flocculate as well it takes longer for the yeast to settle out of the beer. The chilling of the beer also causes haze-forming proteins to coagulate and solidify where they can either settle out of the beer or be filtered out. Even ales can

BELOW: Traditionally beer was fermented in open fermenters such as this one in Belgium.

benefit from at least a few days of near-freezing temperatures to cause the remaining yeast to fall out of suspension.

As mentioned, there are an estimated five hundred compounds derived from yeast that contribute to flavor and aroma, but there are a few whose contribution is worth noting. Certain compounds, such as esters, fusel alcohols, sulfur compounds, acetaldehyde, and diacetyl, can make significant enough contributions that they are worth looking at more closely.

Flavor and Aroma Compounds

Esters

Of all the yeast-derived flavors and aromas, esters have one of the largest impacts on flavor. Esters are responsible for the fruity and floral character of beer and are formed through an enzyme reaction involving an alcohol and a fatty acid. Accordingly, esters are formed after the yeast has started to produce alcohol. Ale strains are known to produce more esters than lager strains, and fermentation conditions such as temperature and availability of nutrients can affect the production of esters. Esters are found in all beer styles, but certain styles such as British ales are known for higher ester levels than other styles such as pilsners.

Fusel Alcohols

While the goal of fermentation is the formation of alcohol, there are many types of alcohols and not all are equal or as desirable. In addition to ethanol, a number of fusel alcohols can be produced as well. Fusel alcohols are formed during the lag phase of fermentation, and can result in warming, hot, or solvent-like flavors in beer. Although large quantities of fusel alcohols are considered an undesirable trait, they exist in quantities above the flavor threshold in many styles of beer. Certain yeast styles produce more fusel alcohols than others, with ale strains generally producing more than lager strains.

Sulfur Compounds

Trace amounts of sulfur compounds can contribute significantly to beer flavor. Although acceptable in small amounts, they can lead to undesirable flavors in excessive amounts requiring prolonged maturation times, or even more aggressive intervention. Sulfur compounds such as hydrogen sulfide and sulfur dioxide are products of yeast fermentation. Much of these compounds is "scrubbed" from the fermenting wort by rising CO_2 bubbles, leading to a rotten egg–like smell, or the smell of a burnt match, during fermentation.

Diacetyl

At low levels, diacetyl can add a slickness to the beer's mouthfeel, and in higher levels it can impart a buttery/butterscotch- or honey/toffee-like flavor. Diacetyl is produced outside of the yeast cell, from precursors that are produced during the lag and growth phases of fermentation. While a low level of diacetyl is usually the goal, certain styles of beer can have elevated levels of diacetyl, and it can be a key flavor component in British ales. During the maturation stage, diacetyl will be further broken down into flavorless compounds.

Acetaldehyde

Acetaldehyde is an intermediary product produced by yeast during the act of alcoholic fermentation. It can impart a flavor that resembles green apple or cider. If given time, acetaldehyde will be converted to ethanol by the yeast. Its presence in beer is usually a sign that the beer has not had a sufficient amount of time to mature. In properly aged beer, acetaldehyde could be an indicator that the beer has been exposed to oxygen, as ethanol will oxidize back to acetaldehyde.

Fermentation Parameters

There are a multitude of yeast strains to choose from, and when you choose one yeast over another you are usually making that choice based upon the flavor profile that you expect the yeast to contribute. Some yeasts ferment clean without making significant flavor contributions, allowing the malt and hops to shine through, while other yeasts make an unmistakable contribution to both the flavor and aroma of the beer. In order to obtain the contribution you expect from the yeast, you have to provide them with the best environment that you can. Considering the contribution that they make to the end product and taking a few basic steps can have a significant impact on the quality of your beer.

A Little Too Much Activity

Occasionally you will come across a particularly vigorous fermentation that pushes the stopper out of the fermentation vessel. The yeast and krausen comes following behind and can leave quite a mess. This can be prevented by using a blow-off tube. A blow-off tube is simply a large diameter tube that fits snugly in the fermenter. The other end is placed in a bucket of water or sanitizer, creating a makeshift airlock. Gas can escape, no oxygen gets back into the fermenter, and any yeast that makes its way out ends up in the bucket.

ABOVE: An extremely vigorous fermentation has the ability to build up pressure in the vessel and cause the stopper and airlock to come out (sometimes violently) and yeast to flow out of the fermenter. This can be prevented by using a blow-off tube.

Pitching Rates

One of the simplest steps that a homebrewer can take to increase the quality of his or her beer is to ensure that he or she is pitching an adequate amount of yeast to the wort. A significant amount of flavor compounds are produced during the growth phase of the yeast. When the yeast is first pitched it begins to take up oxygen and nutrients from the wort and will continue to multiply until it has used up the available nutrients. If you start out with a small number of yeast cells, they will need to produce a greater number of new yeast cells before the available nutrients are used than if you pitched a greater number of yeast cells to start with. As the yeast reproduces it is producing a large number of flavor compounds. A low pitching rate can result in increased esters, diacetyl, acetaldehyde, and low attenuation. There is also a concern with contamination as there is a greater chance that unwanted bacteria could out-compete the yeast resulting in further off-flavors.

There is a possibility of over-pitching, which could result in less than desired production of flavor compounds and aromatics, although it is generally considered better to over-pitch than under-pitch. The real question is how to determine what the proper pitching rate is and how to get there. To determine the amount of yeast to pitch for a 5-gallon batch of beer you can use the following equations for a rough estimate, where SG equals the last two points on your specific gravity reading for the wort. There are two different equations, one for ale yeasts and the other for lager yeasts, as the lager yeasts generally require you to pitch twice as much compared to ale yeasts.

Ales : 3.6 x SG = Yeast Cells in Billions

Lagers : 7.2 x SG = Yeast Cells in Billions

As an example, if you were brewing an ale that was to have a starting specific gravity of 1.048, you would multiply 3.6 by 48, to reach a pitching rate of approximately 173 billion yeast cells. A lager of the same gravity would require 346 billion cells.

The two major suppliers of liquid yeast sell packages that contain approximately 100 billion cells, which they claim is sufficient for wort with gravities up to 1.060. While this number is far less than what the previous calculations would give you, the suppliers claim (perhaps rightfully) that if you have a fresh package of *their* yeast you can be assured that all of the yeast cells are viable whereas the previous calculation assumes a certain percentage of non-viable yeast cells. Furthermore, wort with a gravity over 1.060 is considered to be a high-gravity wort that places a lot of stress on the yeast. At such specific gravities, proper pitch count becomes much more important as the yeast will struggle in such an environment.

In either case it is always a good idea to make a yeast starter. This will increase the amount of yeast that you are pitching, and ensure that the yeast are active when pitched. There are instructions later in this chapter for preparing a starter. In order to determine the size of starter that is needed, there are a number of very good calculators available online that can be found by performing a search for a "pitching rate calculator." One of the best pitching rate calculators that can be found is located at www.mrmalty.com. Mr. Malty is run by Jamil Zainsheff, who has probably done more to promote proper pitching rates than anyone else in the hobby. Even if you are unable to make the recommended size of starter, an undersized starter is always preferable to no starter at all.

Temperature Control

Many would argue that temperature control is the most important facet of fermentation, even more so than pitching rate. Low fermentation temperatures can result in low attenuation or, worse yet, a stuck fermentation. High fermentation temperatures can contribute to the production of fusel alcohols during the lag phase, diacetyl precursors during the growth phase, and increased ester production during active fermentation.

The proper fermentation temperature is dependent on the specific strain of yeast. Generally speaking, ale yeast will ferment properly in a range between 62 and 72 degrees Fahrenheit, with most people aiming for a number somewhere in the middle. Higher temperatures will produce more esters, while lower numbers will produce a cleaner tasting beer. You will find that specific strains will have ranges higher or lower than the average, and thus it is important to look at the manufacturers recommendations. By way of example, yeast strains from Britain, which generally produce more esters, have a tendency to be more tolerant of higher temperatures, while German yeast strains are often more tolerant of lower temperatures.

Lager strains generally require a cooler fermentation temperature, with an average fermentation range between 48 and 58 degrees Fahrenheit. The cooler temperatures of lager fermentation result in a cleaner tasting beer with less esters. As with ale strains, there are exceptions to the recommended ranges, and the manufacturers instructions should always be consulted. For example, yeast strains used for the California Common style (Anchor Steam being the most widely known) are often tolerant of ale-strain fermentation temperatures, which would often kill other lager strains of yeast.

Another thing to consider when monitoring your fermenting wort is that fermentation is an exothermic reaction. The activity of the yeast creates heat and the fermenting wort could have a temperature that is approximately 5 degrees higher than the ambient temperature.

There are many ways—from the really low-tech to the very high-tech—to regulate the temperature of your beer while it is fermenting. Traditionally, beer was brewed with the seasons to take advantage of the weather, and this is still an option depending on where you live, but has the distinct disadvantage of limiting your brewing to certain times of the year.

Depending on your local climate, you may need to either keep your fermenting beer warm or cool it down. Frankly, keeping your beer warm is by far the easier of the two options. There are a number of items on the market similar to electric blankets that wrap around the fermenter that have the ability to not only keep the beer warm but regulate the temperature as well. An inexpensive way to keep your beer warm is to place the fermenter in a large bin filled with water, and then use an aquarium heater to keep the water warm. Aquarium heaters usually come with a built-in thermostat, but make sure to double-check it against another thermometer as they are notoriously inaccurate. The water bin will also help guard against temperature swings, as the water in the bin effectively adds to the thermal mass.

If you need to cool your fermenter there are also a number of options. Once again, placing the fermenter in a bin full of water will help prevent temperature swings. Bottles of ice can be added to the water to help bring the temperature down. If you live in a dry climate, evaporative cooling can be used by placing a T-shirt over the fermenter and directing a fan to blow air across it. The T-shirt will wick water up as the fan continuously causes the water to evaporate, cooling the fermenter in the same way that sweat helps cool your body on a hot day.

Another option is to build a box out of Styrofoam insulation to hold the fermenter and swap out ice bottles. Ice can be a very effective cooling mechanism for fermentation. As the ice bottle cools the ambient air in the box, the fermenter will cool down as well. There are many different designs for these systems, some of them containing multiple compartments with fans to blow cold air from one to another with the aid of a thermostat in order to achieve precise temperature control.

Another option is to use a chest freezer with an external thermostat. Chest freezers can often be found used, and there are a number of digital thermostats available to choose from. The thermostat is necessary as chest freezers do not have the ability to regulate their temperature with any precision above freezing. While such a system has certain space requirements and can be costly, especially if a used freezer cannot be found, it allows precision temperature control that allows not only for ale and lager fermentation but will allow cold crashing and long-term lagering as well.

Yeast Starter

There are many reasons why you might want to use a yeast starter. You can use a starter to increase the amount of yeast for pitching, test yeast viability, or propagate yeast from a bottle conditioned commercial beer. Preparing a yeast starter is an extremely simple thing that can go a long way toward helping you make better beer.

The basic idea is to add your yeast to a small amount of wort and give it some time for fermentation to start. Using this method, you can increase the amount of yeast that you have for pitching come brew day. You can also ensure that the yeast that you have is viable and that you are pitching healthy active yeast. This will allow active fermentation to start sooner, decreasing the chance that a wild yeast (or bacteria) would have the chance to out-compete the yeast of your choice in the wort that you put so much time and effort into creating.

Most often people will make fresh wort using DME. While it doesn't need to be exact, you want to aim for a specific gravity of 1.040. This ensures that there are ample sugars available for the yeast, but that the specific gravity is not so high that it places stress on the yeast. When measuring DME it is best to measure its weight rather than its volume, and in order to reach a SG of 1.040, you want to add approximately 2 ounces of DME to 2 cups of water. (By volume, this works out to slightly less than ½ cup per pint of water.) If you have the ability to measure things out in metric, it is even easier as the ratio is 1 gram of DME to 10 ML of water.

Equipment

The equipment to make a yeast starter is fairly simple and straightforward and, outside of some sanitizer, you may have everything you need already in your kitchen.

- An appropriately sized pot—the pot should be anywhere from 1.5 to 2 times as large as the starter you intend to make.
- Spoon—to mix in the DME and stir the wort.
- Large pot or sink—to use for an ice bath.
- Large glass jar (larger than the amount of starter you want to make)—one with a lid is even better.
- Funnel—to pour the wort into the glass jar.
- Aluminum foil—to cover the starter.
- Sanitizer

Ingredients

As far as ingredients go, you will need your yeast and an appropriate amount of DME. While not necessary, a yeast nutrient can often be helpful.

Procedure

The following instructions are for making a 16-fluid ounce starter. This is a good amount to "proof" the yeast to make sure that it is viable and active when you pitch. If you were attempting to significantly increase the amount of yeast that you were pitching, you would want to use a larger starter, but the procedure would be the same.

I. CLEAN AND SANITIZE

As with everything else in brewing, the first step is to make sure that your equipment is clean. Anything that will come into contact with the wort after it has been boiled will need to be sanitized. This includes the funnel, aluminum foil, and glass jar.

2. BOIL

Bring 2 cups of water to a boil in a quart-sized pot. Once the water has reached a boil, remove the heat and add 2 ounces or ½ cup of DME and stir. Return the heat and bring the wort to a boil. Boil for 10–15 minutes.

BELOW: As with everything else with brewing, cleaning and sanitizing your equipment is very important.

ABOVE: Measuring out DME

3. COOL

Remove the wort from the heat and place it into an ice bath. You can either use a larger pot as seen in the photo, the sink, or whatever else you might have handy. You want to bring the temp of the wort down to about 70 degrees Fahrenheit. I usually cover it and let it sit until it comes to room temp rather than worrying about directly measuring the temperature.

4. PITCH

Pour the wort into the glass jar using the sanitized funnel, and then pour the yeast into the wort. This is a good time to add some yeast nutrient if you have it. Just add it per the manufacturer's instructions.

5. AERATE

Cover the jar with its lid if you have it and shake the wort up in order to adequately aerate it. A few minutes of vigorous shaking will be sufficient. If your jar does not have a lid, you can swir the wort in the jar for several minutes.

6. COVER

Remove the lid from the jar, and replace it with a piece of sanitized aluminum foil. You do not want to use the lid, because the lid will be airtight, and the goal is to allow any CO_2 that is produced to escape.

7. LET SIT

Let the starter sit for 24–48 hours in order to allow fermentation to take place. When fermenting on such a small scale, active fermen-

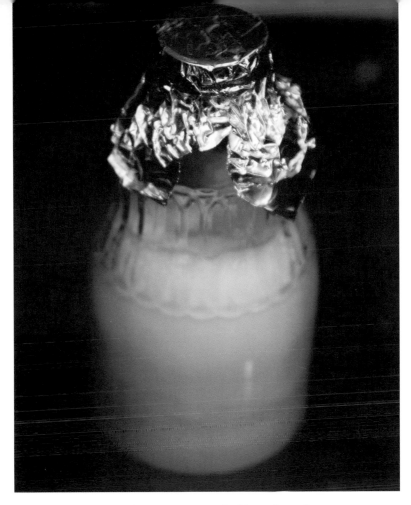

tation can be rather quick and you may miss it. If you don't see active fermentation, you can often tell if you missed it by looking at the sides of the jar as there may be yeast residue and buildup on the sides.

You will want to use the yeast starter as quickly as possible, but it can sit for about a week without a problem. Any longer than that though and you will want to prepare another starter.

Yeast Washing

As I am sure you have noticed by now (assuming you have tried your hand at brewing), there is a thick layer of sediment, or trub, at the bottom of the fermenter when fermentation is complete. If you look closely at the trub through a glass fermenter (i.e., a glass carboy)

ABOVE: At the end of fermentation, yeast along with an assortment of spent grains, hops, proteins, and fats settle out at the bottom of the fermenter. The yeast can be harvested for future use, but it must be separated out from the rest of the materials.

you will notice that the sediment is stratified. The bottom-most portion of the sediment contains spent grains and hops that made their way into the fermenter as well as proteins and fats. The upper portion of the sediment contains yeast that has fallen out of suspension, and it is possible to reuse that yeast in subsequent brews. If you choose to reuse your yeast, the first step you will want to take is to extract the yeast from the other sediment. This process is called yeast washing.

The process is fairly simple. You mix the trub up, pour it into a container of water, and then set it aside. As the trub falls out of suspension the yeast will be the last to fall out. After about an hour, all

An Erlenmeyer flask that has been filled with water and then topped off with the trub from the bottom of a fermenter.

of the heavier particles have fallen out of suspension, and the liquid can be decanted off the heavier particles on the bottom. This decanted liquid is full of yeast, which can be re-pitched into a subsequent brew. The best part of the process is that it doesn't take any special equipment—all that is required are two sanitized containers and the trub from your last brew.

Step 1

The first step, as with most brewing activities, is to make sure that all of your equipment has been cleaned and sanitized. This example uses a large mason jar with a lid and a 2000 milliliter Erlenmeyer flask; although a flask is not necessary, it does make things a bit easier. After cleaning, boil approximately a quart of water for at least 15 minutes in order to make sure that it is sanitized and won't contaminate the yeast. In another pot, boil the two glass jars and at least one lid. This is where an Erlenmeyer flask comes in handy as you can put the flask directly on gas heat and boil the water in the flask. This will

LEFT: After about an hour, three distinct layers are noticeable. The bottom layer is the heavier particles from the trub. The middle layer is the yeast that you want to harvest.

ABOVE: The white line at the top of the sediment is the first yeast starting to fall out of suspension.

make sure the flask and the water in it are sanitized. Once everything is clean and sanitized you will want to let it cool down. After everything has cooled down, fill one of the jars about halfway with the preboiled water.

Step 2

Take the fermenter and mix up the trub by swishing around the small amount of beer that you left behind. If you do not have enough beer left, add a small amount of pre-boiled water to the fermenter in order to loosen up the trub.

Step 3

Pour as much of the trub as you can into the half full jar or flask. Cover the jar with either its lid or a sanitized piece of aluminum foil and mix up the water and trub. Place the jar aside and let it sit for about an hour. During this time, the liquid will

LEFT: The liquid from the flask should be decanted into the second sterilized jar.

After a few days in the refrigerator the yeast will completely settle to the bottom.

Before use, the liquid can be decanted off of the yeast.

start to stratify as the heavier particles begin to fall out of suspension. In the accompanying picture, you can see three distinct layers. The middle layer is full of yeast, while the bottom layer is full of the heavier sediment. The top layer is almost clear of both.

Step 4

After another hour the bottom layer has somewhat compacted. If you look very closely at the sediment you can see a thin layer of a lighter-colored sediment. This is yeast. Once this thin layer has developed it is time to decant the liquid off the rest of the sediment.

Step 5

Slowly, and gently, pour off the liquid into the other clean and sanitized jar. Try as hard as you can to not disturb the layer of sediment on the bottom. Place a lid on the jar, and stick the jar in a refrigerator for storage. There is some debate about how long the yeast can be stored in this manner. There are plenty of stories of people storing yeast like this for months on end. Generally, it is best to use the yeast within a few weeks of washing to ensure that is viable.

Step 6

As the yeast sits in the refrigerator awaiting use, it will continue to fall out of suspension. Before use, the liquid can be decanted from the yeast cake on the bottom of the jar. Pour the yeast slurry from the bottom of the jar into a starter. If the yeast is being used within a week or so of washing, and if you obtained enough of it you can pitch this directly into your next brew.

PART III

Trouble-Shooting

occasions when things do not go as planned: The beer tastes funny or has a bad aroma. Perhaps it is hazy, or instead of a nice fluffy white head, it never builds or it dissipates quickly. Perhaps the beer is flat, or comes gushing out the top as soon as the bottle is opened. More often than you would expect, allowing the beer a bit more time to mature will rectify many problems. There are very few times when you will need to actually give up on a beer. If it has an off-flavor, or just does not taste the way you would expect, putting the beer aside for a few weeks can clean up off-flavors. Of course there are defects that no amount of time will correct, but those can always be dumped (only in truly extreme circumstances) after you have given it time to self correct.

⑩
Common Off-Flavors and Aromas

OCCASIONALLY, DESPITE YOUR best efforts, your final product may have unwanted flavors and aromas. These can usually be traced back to specific errors that were made during brewing and fermentation. By recognizing the cause of an unwelcome flavor or aroma you can make adjustments to prevent it from happening again.

Alcohol/Hot

While alcohol presence is a crucial element in any beer, it should never taste like a solvent, or paint thinner. Excessive alcohol presence is sometimes referred to as "hotness" and usually occurs from unusually high fermentation temperatures. Fermentation temperatures should not be kept above 80 degrees Fahrenheit. Sharp alcoholic flavors may also occur from under-pitching.

Apple Cider/Wine

Cidery flavors and aromas often resemble the flavors and aromas of apple cider or sometimes wine. It is possible that it is caused by using too much sugar in a recipe although this is debatable. It can also be caused by using old or stale extract or infection by aceto bacteria.

Bitter/Mouth Puckering

While a bitter flavor derived from hops can be desirable, astringent, mouth-puckering flavors are not. They are often dry, bitter, and can be powdery. They are caused by tannin extraction due to over-steeping, over-sparging, or sparging at too hot a temperature. They can also be caused by over-milled grains or a mash pH that exceeds the range of 5.2–5.6. Don't over-hop in the bittering or finishing stages as this will also produce high levels of astringency.

Bread

Yeasty flavors and aromas resemble that of bread. If the yeast begins to cannibalize, it will produce yeasty off-flavors. Young beers will often have a yeasty character as well as beer that has been improperly decanted. Make sure you leave the yeast in the bottom of the bottle when you pour a homebrew. If you still taste yeast, give it a little more time to mature.

Butter/Butterscotch

A butter or butterscotch smell or taste is often caused by diacetyl, which can often be detected by the slick feel it produces in the mouth. While diacetyl is acceptable in small amounts in certain styles, it is often an unwanted characteristic in a given brew. It is produced naturally during the early stages of fermentation and becomes reabsorbed by the yeast toward the end of the fermentation process. If the yeast is weak or highly flocculated then the diacetyl might not be absorbed properly. It can also be caused by short boils, bacterial infections, or relatively low fermentation temperatures. Diacetyl will be broken down to tasteless compounds as long as the beer is still in contact with the yeast—allow the beer time to mature, and don't rack the beer off of the yeast cake too quickly.

Cooked Vegetables/ Shellfish

Dimethyl sulfide (DMS) resembles the flavors and aromas of shellfish or cooked vegetables, particularly corn and cabbage. Although it is acceptable and desired in some styles, it is generally ill-advised to have high levels. DMS is produced in hot wort and removed naturally with evaporation in the boil. A strong vigorous boil will drive off DMS and cooling the wort quickly will prevent further buildup. It may also be caused by a bacterial infection due to poor sanitization and will be particularly rancid smelling in such a case.

Fruit/Banana

Esters are a natural by-product of fermentation and produce fruity aromas and flavors, especially banana. Again, while it is an acceptable and desired characteristic of some styles, it is not preferred in others. Some yeast strains yield higher levels, and it should be noted that higher temperatures produce more esters.

Grass

Grassy or musty aromas and flavors can be attributed to poor product preservation and storage. In most cases, ingredients that haven't been packaged or stored properly will develop bacteria and molds that produce grassy smells. Grassy flavor can also be picked up from hops, if the beer is allowed to dry hop for too long.

Green Apples/Pumpkin

Acetaldehyde in a brew will give off the flavor and aroma of green apples or pumpkin. While the presence of acetaldehyde might indicate a bacterial infection, chances are that the brew is simply too young and must age and condition to allow time enough for the yeast to convert the overabundance of acetaldehyde into ethanol. Maturation can often fix this problem. Acetaldehyde can also be created when alcohol is allowed to oxidize, so care must be taken when bottling not to allow the beer to become aerated.

Husk/Grain

Husk and grain aromas and flavors are comparable to astringent ones. Using over-milled grains and highly toasted malts are often the culprits. Preventing astringent flavors will usually prevent husky flavors as well.

Metal

Metallic flavors are often produced from the leeching of iron, aluminum, or steel from pots or other pieces of metallic equipment into the wort during the boiling process. They are also sometimes caused by poorly stored or packaged malts.

Mold

Mold causes mildew and musty aromas and flavors. Ingredients should be checked thoroughly prior to brewing as well as equipment. Ferment in a dry, dark place rather than in a damp and humid atmosphere.

Paper

Oxidation produces a variety of flavors and aromas including cardboard, sherry, old, stale, papery, and bitterness. Oxidation mainly occurs with excessive splashing of the wort or exposure to outside air, which should be avoided once the beer has fermented.

Paint Thinner

Solvent flavors and aromas are similar to ester and alcoholic off-flavors. They usually resemble paint thinner or nail polish remover and are harsh in the mouth. These off-flavors usually occur due to a combination of oxidation and relatively high fermentation temperatures. Nonfood-grade plastic equipment can also leech solvent-esque flavors and aromas into the brew.

Plastic/Medicine

Chlorophenol produces plastic, iodine, or medicine-like aromas and flavors. This is caused by cleaning equipment or sparging with chlorinated water. Always use sanitized or filtered water.

Rotten Eggs

Sulfur flavors and aromas smell and taste like burning matches and rotten eggs. While hydrogen sulfide is inevitably produced during fermentation, it is often rendered undetectable after fermentation is complete and is more pronounced with lager yeasts. These off-flavors can be caused by a bacterial infection in the yeast.

Salt

Salt tastes and smells like just what it is: salt. Avoid adding more salt to the recipe until the original salt contents can be established.

Skunk

Skunk flavors and aromas can also smell like burned rubber or cat-musk. Skunkiness is usually caused by the interaction of UV rays and hops. When this interaction occurs, the alpha acids are converted into mercaptan, which is actually one of the chemicals that skunks secrete. Brown bottles protect against UV rays and are strongly suggested and preferred over green and clear containers.

Soap

Soapy flavors and aromas, while sometimes caused by soap in the equipment, are usually produced by keeping the brew in the primary fermenter for too long a period of time. If kept in the fermenter too long after primary fermentation is complete, fatty acids begin to break down and quite literally turn into soap.

Sour

Sour flavors and aromas generally resemble vinegar. While sourness is an element in particular beer styles, when it is not planned or appropriate, it is usually a result of a bacterial infection.

Sweet

Sweetness smells and tastes like sugar. While some amount of sweetness is desirable in most beers, it needs to be balanced by the bitterness of hops. Overwhelmingly sweet beers are often a product of stuck fermentation.

*   *   *

It is important to realize that all of these potential problems can be overcome by paying attention to your process. Proper cleaning and sanitation practices, along with providing the yeast a proper environment to work in, will go a long way toward preventing problems in the first place. When problems do arise, find the root of the problem and learn from your mistake and the problem is unlikely to occur again.

HAZE

What causes haze?

Haze generally occurs from one or two possible causes.
1. Suspended particles of proteins and yeast
2. Bacterial infections

How can I clarify beer that has a bacterial infection?

If you have a bacterial infection, there is no remedy. Keep all of your equipment clean and sanitized, including post-brewing tools and brewing area. Also monitor how long your wort has been sitting both before and after fermentation. Stagnant brew can become a breeding ground for mold and bacteria.

Is haze acceptable in beer?

Haze can be acceptable, and there are many styles where haze is a predominant characteristic of the beer and there are many styles where haze will not be noticeable. But not all styles allow for haze. It is important to keep in mind that homebrewers, as opposed to commercial breweries, often use natural methods of carbonation. As such, live yeast must remain in the brew to activate fermentation and, thus, natural carbonation. This method generally produces haze-making materials. Whether you find haze an unfortunate by-product or completely acceptable, there are methods available in order to clarify your brew.

How can I clarify haze?

1. Protein (or Protease) Rest

All-malt beers are particularly prone to haze, but all beer is susceptible. A solution is to stabilize the mash temperature at about 122 degrees Fahrenheit for a period of time in order to allow optimum enzyme production, particularly of the kind that break down proteins, thus reducing haze-making particles.

2. Rolling Boils and Quick Chills

Boiling the wort heavily for a long period of time as compared with a weak, short boil can produce significantly more break material resulting in a clearer brew. Similarly, chilling the wort as quickly as possible also results in significantly more break material, removing heavy, light-reflecting proteins. When siphoning, or transferring, the wort into a secondary container, be sure to decant properly leaving the break material and trub at the bottom of the primary container.

3. Finings

There are many varieties of finings that, when used in combination with these other methods, will enhance beer clarity. Finings work by attracting haze-forming proteins and causing them to clump together so they settle out of the beer faster or are able to be filtered out.

COLLOIDAL SILICA: Available in liquid suspension form, and able to be combined with the use of gelatin to accelerate yeast flocculation.

DIATOMACEOUS EARTH: A naturally occurring sedimentary rock composed of the skeletal remains of single-celled plants that is generally available in powder form. For brewing, it is a main component in certain filter systems.

GELATIN: The colder the beer, the better gelatin works. It combines with tannic acids which then adhere to yeast and protein particles, dropping them out of the wort. It is important to note that gelatin is made from animal skin, bones, and hooves. Kosher-observant and most vegetarian beer lovers will not drink beer that has been clarified with gelatin.

IRISH MOSS (CARRAGEENAN): A natural additive, Irish moss is a seaweed that has a naturally negative charge and is sold in flake form. As such, the positively charged proteins are attracted to the flakes and clump together, sinking to the bottom of the wort.

ISINGLASS: Made from the swim bladder of fish, and available in a variety of forms, it accelerates the flocculation of yeast causing it to sink in the wort. It is usually added near completion of the entire brewing process. It is important to note that some vegetarians find this fining an unacceptable additive.

PECTINASE: An enzyme that can be extracted from certain fungi that breaks down plant material, particularly fruits, and pectin, a haze-causing material.

PVPP (POLYVINYLPOLYPYRROLIDONE): Used as a binding agent, PVPP is a very quick and effective powdered plastic that uses static electricity to bind impurities such as protein, yeast, and polyphenol particles, to itself.

⑫
HEAD RETENTION

THERE ARE A few reasons why your beer may not have stable head retention. Those reasons include low carbonation, a presence of fats in your ingredients or equipment, high levels of protein-attacking enzymes, or high alcohol levels. Essentially, brews with high levels of proteins and hops usually have better head retention. However, there are several methods that you as a homebrewer can use to facilitate better head retention in your beer.

1. Soap

Household soaps and detergents significantly reduce head retention. Use cleaners available from your homebrew supplier on equipment, bottles, and glassware. If you use soap on your glassware, make sure you rinse it well.

2. Glassware

Use it correctly! Beer glasses are designed to facilitate good head retention for their particular style. Short wide glasses reduce head retention, which is why most are tall, narrow, or tapered.

3. Hops

High alpha acid content produces better head retention. The hoppier your brew, the better the foam.

4. Malts

Crystal and caramel malts often enhance body and head retention. This is because they are full of heavy proteins which help to produce nice foam. On the other hand, high levels of proteins in a brew can lead to haze.

5. Heading Agents

Available at your homebrew supplies provider, heading agents are added into a brew by individualized directions. Make sure to follow the manufacturer's directions as they vary by product. It is important to note that these agents will often change the character of the beer so use caution when choosing this option.

6. Protein Rests

As protein leads to better foam formation, allowing them to break down during a protein rest can potentially reduce head retention in the finished product. Depending on what you want the finished product to look like, be cautious of your mashing schedule and temperatures.

7. Adjuncts

The following is a list of head-enhancing grains. For more detailed information, please see the adjunct table on page 193.
- Raw Barley
- Flaked Oats
- Flaked Wheat
- Torrefied Wheat

THERE ARE A number of problems that can arise during bottling. They are usually the result of improper carbonation. The fixes are simple, and the problems are unlikely to occur again once you have addressed the underlying cause.

⑬
BOTTLING PROBLEMS

Flat Beer

Occasionally, you will have bottles or entire batches of beer that do not carbonate properly. If it is the entire batch, you may have forgotten to add priming sugar. While this sounds unlikely, it does happen. The other possibility is that carbonation has simply not completed. For one reason or another (such as the beer being too cold during the carbonation period), the yeast has not finished. As such, it is always best to give the beer another week before taking any corrective action.

If it is just a few bottles that are flat, it can be one of two problems. If the bottle is completely flat (i.e., there is absolutely no carbonation), the cap may not have properly sealed the bottle. If the beer is slightly carbonated, you may not have properly mixed in the priming sugar during bottling time. As a result, the sugar was not evenly distributed between all of the bottles. If this happened, you will find that while some bottles are relatively flat others are overcarbonated.

If your beer failed to carbonate, you can try adding a measured amount of priming sugar directly to each bottle. Using corn sugar, you can add approximately ½ teaspoon per 12-ounce bottle or 1 teaspoon per 22-ounce bottle. Some homebrew shops carry premeasured sugar tablets that can be used as well.

If your beer is undercarbonated, it is best not to try and fix the problem. You risk overcarbonating the beer, which could cause the beer to foam up when the bottle is opened or, worse yet, explode from too much pressure.

Gushers

There are a number of reasons why the beer will gush when the bottle is opened. The usual culprit is too much priming sugar. Either too much priming sugar was added to the whole batch, or the priming sugar was not evenly distributed during bottling. If it's the latter, some bottles will be undercarbonated.

The other possibility is that the beer has a bacterial infection, which caused more pressure to build up in the bottle than if yeast were acting upon the beer alone. Often the beer will have a bad aroma if bacteria is to blame. If it smells funny, dump the beer; otherwise it is fine to drink.

In either case, there is little that can be done to rectify the situation except to be more careful the next time around.

Bottle Bombs

Don't be alarmed, but bottles of homebrew have been known to occasionally explode. For the same reasons that you could end up with a gusher (overcarbonation or a bacterial infection), the pressure could build up so much that the bottle cannot maintain its integrity and it explodes. This usually happens with thinner bottles, but can occur with heavier bottles too.

As with gushers, little can be done to rectify the situation except to be more careful the next time. Make sure that you are using good sanitation procedures, and that you are thoroughly mixing the correct amount of the priming sugar.

APPENDIX A

Adjuncts

TECHNICALLY, AN ADJUNCT is any source of fermentable sugars that cannot self-convert. In homebrewing the term is used more liberally, and encompasses not only non-self-converting sugars but most any other additive as well. The following adjuncts are used in homebrewing, and the table indicates whether they need to be mashed or not. The maximum percentage of use is based upon the ability of the base grains to supply enough enzymes for conversion.

	Name	Effect on Finished Beer	Requires Mash?	Maximum Percentage of Grain Bill
BARLEY	Flaked Barley	Increases residual sugar to aid in mouth-feel	Yes	20
	Raw Barley	Imparts a grainy, fuller-bodied flavor and increases head retention.	Yes	15
	Torrefied Barley	Increases the body, like raw barley, but has a higher yield.	Yes	40

	Name	Effect on Finished Beer	Requires Mash?	Maximum Percentage of Grain Bill
CORN	Corn Starch	Lightens body.	Yes	10
	Flaked Corn	Produces a beer with a less earthy flavor and lightens color and body.	Yes	40
	Torrefied Corn	Has the same effect as corn grits and flaked corn, lightening the body of the beer, but has a higher yield than flaked corn.	Yes	40
GRITS	Corn Grits	Decreases the protein content thus lightening the body of the beer. It also imparts a grainy, corn-like taste.	Yes	10
	Rice Grits	Lightens the body of the beer without changing the smell or flavor.	Yes	10
	Sorghum Grits	Lightens the body of the beer slightly and increases stability.	Yes	45
OATS	Flaked Oats	Extends longevity of beer foam and increases body.	Yes	30
OTHER	Acorn	Produces a woodsy and full-bodied taste.	Yes	15
	Caramel	Imparts a sweet caramel flavor and a color between amber and dark brown.	No	15
	Chocolate	Provides a dark color and a nutty, chocolaty flavor.	No	To taste
	Coffee	Imparts a rich coffee flavor.	No	5

	Name	Effect on Finished Beer	Requires Mash?	Maximum Percentage of Grain Bill
	Corn Syrup	Increases alcohol content with limited effect on flavor	No	10
	Fruit	Imparts a fruity flavor.	Optional	Varied
	Honey	Softens the body and imparts a sweet and dry flavor.	No	30
	Maple Syrup	Creates a smoky, dry flavor if added during the boil, or a smoother maple taste when added after.	No	10
	Molasses	Imparts sweetness and smoothness.	No	5
	Oak Chips	Imparts an oaky, barrel-aged taste.	No	Varied
	Potato	Lightens both beer flavor and color.	Yes	20
	Sorghum Starch	Lightens beer slightly and increases stability.	Yes	45
	Spices	Imparts the flavor of whatever spice used.	Optional	Varied
RICE	Flaked Rice	Does not affect the basic flavor of the beer, but adds crispness.	Yes	25
RYE	Flaked Rye	Imparts a distinct and sharp flavor.	Yes	10
SUGAR	Brown Sugar	Adds sweetness and richness to beer.	No	10
	Candi Sugar (Clear, Amber and Dark)	Increases alcohol content without overly sweetening, and sweetens the beer's aroma.	No	7

	Name	Effect on Finished Beer	Requires Mash?	Maximum Percentage of Grain Bill
	Cane Sugar (Beet Sugar)	Sweetens, and decreases body of the beer.	No	7
	Demerera Sugar	Smoothes and sweetens the beer.	No	10
	Invert Sugar	Increases the alcohol content with limited effect on taste.	No	10
	Milk Sugar (Lactose)	Imparts a very sweet taste and a creamy texture.	No	10
	Rice Sugar	Slightly softens the body of the beer and increases alcohol content.	No	10
	Table Sugar	Lightens the color and softens the body of the beer. Is a mild sweetener.	No	10
	Turbinado (Raw Sugar)	Sweetens the beer.	No	10
WHEAT	Flaked Wheat	Adds body and a wheat flavor to the beer while increasing foam content and stability. Has a flavor sometimes described as dry.	Yes	40
	Torrefied Wheat	Has the same effect as flaked wheat, increasing foam and body, but a higher yield.	Yes	40
	Wheat Starch	Similar to corn grits, it lightens the body of the beer and imparts a slight wheat taste.	Yes	40

APPENDIX B

Hops

* Noble hops varieties

** Goldings are available in a variety of strains, including East Kent Goldings, Kent Goldings, and Styrian Goldings.

	NAME	USE	ORIGIN	AA %	SUBSTI-TUTES	DESCRIP-TION
A	**Admiral**	Bittering	England	11.0–16.2	Challenger; Northdown; Target	citrus, orange
	Ahtanum	Aroma	USA (Yakima, WA)	5.7–6.3	Amarillo; Cascade	citrus, earthy, floral
	Amarillo	Aroma	USA (Toppenish, WA)	8.0–11.0	Ahtanum; Cascade; Centennial; Chinook	floral, orange, spicy
	Apollo	Bittering	USA (Prosser, WA)	18.0–21.0	Magnum; Columbus	orange, spicy

	NAME	USE	ORIGIN	AA %	SUBSTI-TUTES	DESCRIP-TION
	Aquila	Aroma	USA	6.0–7.5	Cluster	Commercially discontinued
B	Bobeck	Both	Slovenia	3.5–7.0	Styrian Goldings	citrus
	Bramling Cross	Both	England	5.0–7.0	Kent Goldings; Progress; Whitbread Golding	black currant, lemon
	Bravo	Bittering	USA	14.0–17.0	Columbus	earthy, floral, fruity, spicy
	Brewer's Gold	Bittering	England	6.0–10.0	Bullion; Galena	black currant, spicy
	Bullion	Bittering	England	6.5–9.0	Brewer's Gold; Columbus; Galena; Northern Brewer	black currant, earthy, spicy
C	Cascade	Both	USA (Corvallis, OR)	4.0–7.1	Ahtanum; Amarillo; Centennial	citrus, grapefruit
	Centennial	Both	USA	9.0–12.0	Amarillo; Cascade; Chinook; Columbus	citrus
	Challenger	Both	England	6.3–10.0	Northern Brewer; Perle	resiny, spicy
	Chinook	Bittering	USA	11.0–4.0	Eroica; Galena; Nugget	piney, spicy

NAME	USE	ORIGIN	AA %	SUBSTITUTES	DESCRIPTION
Citra	Both	USA	10.0–12.0	Amarillo; Centennial; Columbus	citrus, tropical fruits
Cluster	Both	USA	5.5–8.5	Brewer's Gold, Chinook, Galena	spicy
Columbia	Aroma	USA (Corvallis, OR)	6.8–11.5	Willamette	Commercially discontinued
Columbus	Both	USA	12.0–16.0	Chinook; Centennial; Northern Brewer; Nugget; Target	citrus, woody
Comet	Bittering	USA (Corvallis, OR)	9.4–12.4	Galena	Commercially discontinued
Crystal	Aroma	USA (Corvallis, OR)	3.0–4.5	Hallertau; Hersbrucker; Liberty; Mount Hood	black pepper, cinnamon, floral, nutmeg
E **Eroica**	Bittering	USA	11.0–14.0	Galena	Commercially discontinued
F **Falconer's Flight**	Both	USA	10.0–12.0	N/A	citrus, floral, fruity
First Gold	Aroma	England	6.0–9.0	Crystal; Kent Goldings	apricot, citrus, spicy

	NAME	USE	ORIGIN	AA %	SUBSTI-TUTES	DESCRIP-TION
	Fuggles	Aroma	England	4.0–5.5	Styrian Golding; Willamette	earthy, herbal, spicy
G	Galaxy	Both	Australia	13.0–14.8	Centennial; Simcoe	citrus, passion fruit
	Galena	Bittering	USA (Idaho)	12.0–14.0	Nugget	fruity, herbal
	Glacier	Aroma	USA	5.0–6.0	Fuggles; Willamette	citrus, earthy
	Goldings**	Aroma	England; USA	4.0–5.5	Goldings; Progress	floral
	Green Bullet	Bittering	New Zealand	11.0–14.0	Crystal; Hallertau; Liberty; Mount Hood, Ultra	floral, fruity, resiny
H	Hallertau*	Aroma	Germany	3.5–7.0	Hersbrucker; Liberty; Mount Hood	spicy
	Hersbrucker*	Aroma	Germany	2.5–5.0	Hallertau; Mount Hood	earthy, spicy
	Horizon	Both	USA (Oregon)	10.9–15.5	Magnum	citrus, spicy
L	Liberty	Aroma	USA	3.0–5.0	Hallertau; Mount Hood	resiny, spicy
	Lublin	Aroma	Poland	3.0–5.0	Saaz	spicy, woody
M	Magnum	Bittering	Germany	12.0–14.0	N/A	citrus, spicy

NAME	USE	ORIGIN	AA %	SUBSTI-TUTES	DESCRIP-TION
Millennium	Bittering	USA	14.0–16.5	Nugget	floral, resiny, spicy
Motueka	Both	New Zealand	6.5–7.5	Saaz	citrus
Mount Hood	Aroma	USA	4.0–8.0	Crystal; Hallertau; Liberty	spicy, earthy
Mount Rainier	Both	USA (Oregon)	6.0–8.0	Fuggles; Hallertau	floral, spicy
Nelson Sauvin	Bittering	New Zealand (Nelson)	12.0–13.0	N/A	fruity, passion fruit
Newport	Bittering	USA (Corvallis, OR)	10.0–17.0	Galena	resiny
Northdown	Both	England	7.0–10.0	Challenger; Northern Brewer	fruity, spicy
Northern Brewer	Both	England	7.0–10.0	Chinook; Northern Brewer	earthy, woody, fruity
Nugget	Bittering	USA	12.0–16.0	Chinook; Columbus; Galena; Magnum	floral, resiny
Olympic	Bittering	USA	10.0–13.0	Chinook	citrus, spicy
Pacific Gem	Bittering	New Zealand	13.0–15.0	N/A	blackberry, fruity, woody
Pacific Jade	Bittering	New Zealand	12.0–14.0	N/A	black pepper, citrus
Pacifica	Aroma	New Zealand	5.0–6.0	N/A	orange marmalade

	NAME	USE	ORIGIN	AA %	SUBSTI-TUTES	DESCRIP-TION
	Palisade	Both	USA	5.5–10.0	Glacier	apricot, floral
	Perle	Both	Germany	5.0–9.0	Northern Brewer	floral, fruity, spicy
	Phoenix	Both	England (Kent)	8.0–12.0	Challenger	spicy
	Pilgrim	Both	England	9.0–13.0	Target	earthy, spicy
	Pilot	Bittering	England	8.0–12.0	N/A	herbal, lemon
	Pioneer	Both	England	8.0–10.0	Herald	citrus
	Pride of Ringwood	Bittering	Australia	7.0–10.0	Cluster	earthy, herbal
	Progress	Aroma	England	5.0–8.0	Fuggles; Goldings	fruity, resiny, spicy
R	**Rakau**	Both	New Zealand	9.0–11.0	N/A	passion fruit, peach, fruity
	Riwaka	Aroma	New Zealand	4.5–6.5	N/A	grapefruit
S	**Saaz***	Aroma	Czech Republic	2.5–4.5	Tettnang	cinnamon, earthy, spicy
	Santiam	Aroma	USA	5.0–7.0	Tettnang	floral, spicy
	Saphir	Aroma	Germany	2.5–4.5	Hallertau	citrus, tangerine
	Simcoe	Both	USA	11.9–14.0	Cascade	citrus, woody
	Sorachi Ace	Bittering	Japan	10.7–16.0	N/A	lemon

NAME	USE	ORIGIN	AA %	SUBSTI-TUTES	DESCRIP-TION
Southern Cross	Bitter-ing	New Zea-land	11.0–14.0	N/A	lemon, spicy, woody
Spalt*	Aroma	Germany	3.2–6.0	Hallertau; Saaz; Tettnang	spicy, woody
Sterling	Both	USA	6.0–9.0	Mount Hood; Saaz	floral, herbal, spicy
Stickle-bract	Bitter-ing	New Zea-land	12.0–14.0	N/A	citrus, woody
Stris-selspalt	Aroma	France (Alsace)	3.0–5.0	Crystal; Hers-brucker; Mount Hood	floral, lemon
Summit	Bitter-ing	USA	17.0–19.5	Simcoe	grapefruit, orange, tangerine
Super Alpha	Both	New Zea-land	10.0–12.0	N/A	herbal, woody
Target	Both	England	8.0–12.5	Fuggles; Wil-lamette	apple, woody
Tettnang*	Both	Germany	3.5–5.0	Saaz; Spalt	floral, spicy, woody
Toma-hawk (Trade name for Colum-bus)	Both	USA	12.0–16.0	Chinook; Centen-nial; Northern Brewer; Nugget; Target	citrus, woody
Tradition	Aroma	Germany	5.0–7.0	Hallertau; Liberty	spicy

	NAME	USE	ORIGIN	AA %	SUBSTI-TUTES	DESCRIP-TION
U	Ultra	Aroma	USA	3.0–5.0	Crystal; Saaz; Tettnang	floral, spicy
V	Vanguard	Aroma	USA	4.0–6.0	Hallertau; Liberty	citrus, floral
W	Warrior	Bitter-ing	USA	14.0–17.0	Colum-bus; Nugget	citrus, earthy
	Whit-bread Golding Variety (WVG)	Both	England	5.0–7.5	Goldings	fruity
	Wil-lamette	Aroma	USA	3.4–6.0	Fuggles; Goldings	earthy, flo-ral, fruity, spicy
Z	Zeus (Colum-bus; Toma-hawk)	Both	USA	12.0–16.0	Chinook; Centen-nial; Northern Brewer; Nugget; Target	citrus, woody

APPENDIX C

U.S. Homebrewing Laws

HOMEBREWING IS FEDERALLY legal as long as the home-brewer adheres to the limitations addressed in the United States Code of Federal Regulations Title 27, Part 25, Subpart L, Section 25.205 and Section 25.206. Basically, if you are old enough to drink, you are old enough to brew as long as you are over 18. You are allowed to produce and distribute for family or recreational activities although the sale of homebrew is not permitted. In a household with two adults, production cannot exceed 200 gallons. It follows that a household with a single adult cannot exceed 100 gallons. However, according to the 21st amendment, the responsibility and right to regulate alcohol belongs to the states. As such, each state has instituted its own legislation on alcoholic beverages.

*States with an asterisk are those under direct jurisdiction of Alcoholic Beverage Control (ABC). Each state's ABC agency is dedicated to the regulation of production, distribution, and sales of alcoholic beverages within state lines.

NABCA—National Alcohol Beverage Control Association
4401 Ford Avenue, Suite 700
Alexandria, VA 22302-1473
Phone: 703-578-4200
Fax: 703-820-3551
www.nabca.org

Please note that these laws are subject to change, and do change often. As of June 2011, these are the current statutes for each state. If you have any further questions or concerns, please contact your state alcoholic beverage commission.

Alabama* Alabama Alcoholic Beverage Control Board 2715 Gunter Park Drive West Montgomery, Alabama 36109 Mailing Address: P.O. Box 1151 Montgomery, AL 36101 Phone: (334) 271-3840 www.abc.alabama.gov	Prohibited. Homebrew is illegal. There are brewpubs which have recently been established but remain under tight supervision.
Alaska Alcoholic Beverage Control Board 5848 E. Tudor Road Anchorage, AK 99507 Phone: (907) 269-0350	Permitted. Subject to federal and local option laws. Meaning, areas not under the jurisdiction of the local laws of their given communities are subjected to federal law. In some areas, homebrew may be considered illegal under local option laws.
Arizona Arizona Department of Liquor Licenses and Control 800 W. Washington 5th Floor Phoenix, AZ 85007 Phone: (602) 542-5141	Permitted. Subject to federal law. Those with a still or distilling apparatus must register with the state ABC director.

Arkansas Alcohol Beverage Control 1515 W. Seventh Street Room 503 Little Rock, AR 72201 Phone: (501) 682-1105	Permitted. Subject to federal law. The sale of homebrew is also permitted with a permit from the state ABC director. Without a permit, sale is prohibited but homebrew then remains untaxed.
California California Department of Alcoholic Beverage Control 3927 Lennane Drive Suite 100 Sacramento, CA 95834 Phone: (916) 419-2500 California Board of Equalization 450 N. Street Sacramento, CA 94279-0073 Phone: (916) 445-6464	Permitted. Homebrewers must be at least 21 years of age. Limits coincide with federal law.
Colorado Colorado Department of Revenue-Liquor Enforcement Division 1881 Pierce 108A Lakewood, CO 80214-1495 Mailing Address 1375 Sherman Street Denver, CO 80261 Phone: (303) 205-2300	Permitted. Subject to federal law.
Connecticut Connecticut Department of Consumer Protection Liquor Division State Office Building 165 Capitol Ave Hartford, CT 06106 Phone: (860) 713-6200	Permitted. The age of the homebrewer must be at least 21 years of age. A 2-adult household is permitted to produce 100 gallons. A single-adult household is permitted to produce 50 gallons.

Delaware Delaware Department of Public Services Alcoholic Beverage Control Commission Carvel State Office Building 3rd Floor 820 N. French Street Wilmington, DE 19801 Phone: (302) 577-5210 Toll Free: (800) 273-9500	Permitted. Any household with at least one adult may produce up to 200 gallons per calendar year. Consumption laws coincide with federal laws.
Florida Florida Department of Professional Business Regulations Division of Alcoholic Beverages and Tobacco 1940 N. Monroe Tallahassee, FL 32399-0783 Phone: (850) 488-3227	Permitted. Homebrewers must be at least 21 years of age.
Georgia Georgia Department of Revenue Alcohol & Tobacco Tax Division 1800 Century Center Blvd. N.E. Room 4235 Atlanta, GA 30345-3205 Mailing Address: P.O. Box 49728 Atlanta, GA 30359 Phone: (404) 417-4900	Permitted. Households may only produce 50 gallons per calendar year. Anything more requires a permit. Must be used for personal consumption.
Hawaii Honolulu Liquor Commission City and County of Honolulu Pacific Park Plaza 711 Kapiolani Blvd Suite 600 Honolulu, HI 96813 Phone: (808) 523-4458 Toll Free: (800) 838-9976	

Hawaii Department of Liquor Control County of Hawaii 101 Aupuni Street Suite 230 Hilo, HI 96766 Phone: East HI: 961-8218 West HI: 327-3549 **Kauai** Department of Liquor Control County of Kauai Lihue Civic Center Mo'ikeha Building 4444 Rice Street Suite 120 Kauai, III 96766 Phone: (808) 241-6580 **Maui** Department of Liquor Control County of Maui 2145 Kaohu Street Room 107 Wailuku, HI 96793 Phone: (808) 243-7753	Permitted. Households may produce 100 gallons of homebrew per calendar year.
Idaho* Alcohol Beverage Control Bureau 700 South Stratford Drive Suite 115 Meridian, ID 83642 Phone: (208) 884-7060 Toll Free: (888) 222-1360 www.isp.idaho.gov/abc	Permitted. The homebrewer must only use native grown products in the homebrew process. Homebrew is limited to private use. Must not be brewed for sale or public consumption.
Illinois Illinois Liquor Control Commission 100 West Randolph Street Suite 5-300 Chicago, IL 60601 Phone: (312) 814-2206 Springfield Address: 101 West Jefferson Suite 3-525 Springfield, IL 62702 Phone: (217) 782-2136	Permitted. Any product of fermentation is acceptable as long as it remains free of the distillation process.

Indiana Alcohol and Tobacco Commission Indiana Government Ctr. South 302 W. Washington St. Room E-114 Indianapolis, IN 46204 Phone: (317) 232-2430	Permitted. Although previously illegal, the transportation of homebrew is now acceptable. Homebrew limits coincide with federal limits.
Iowa* Iowa Alcoholic Beverages Division 1918 SE Hulsizer Road Ankeny, IA 50021 Phone: (515) 281-7400 Toll Free: (866) 469-2223 www.iowaabd.com	Possibly Permitted. Iowa's statute is ambiguous in its reference to homebrew. It is legal to bottle your own beer for private consumption but illegal to bottle your own beer in order to sell it. We can assume that the manufacture of homebrew would then be legal.
Kansas Kansas Department of Revenue Alcohol Beverage Control Alcohol Beverage Control 915 S.W. Harrison Street Room 214 Topeka, KS 66625-3512 Phone: (785) 296-7015 TTY: (785) 296-6117	Permitted. Consumption is limited to the homebrewer and his/her family. Fermentation is acceptable as long as it remains free of the distillation process.
Kentucky Kentucky Alcoholic Beverage Control Department 1003 Twilight Trail Suite A-2 Frankfort, KY 40601 Phone: (502) 564-4850	Permitted. Subject to federal law. Consumption is limited to the homebrewer and his/her family. It can also be transported to a place with a license to sell alcohol for homebrew competitions, etc.
Louisiana Louisiana Department of Revenue Alcohol and Tobacco Control Office 8549 United Plaza Boulevard Suite 220 Baton Rouge, LA 70809 Phone: (225) 925-4041	Possibly Permitted. Although the manufacture and distribution of alcoholic beverages requires an annual permit, homebrew is not specifically cited in Louisiana legislation.

Maine* Department of Public Safety Liquor Licensing and Compliance 164 State House Station Augusta, ME 04333 Phone: (207) 626-3800 www.maine.gov/dps/liqr	Permitted. Homebrewers must be at least 21 years of age. Limits coincide with federal law. All beer must be brewed for personal consumption and not for sale.
Maryland* Alcohol and Tobacco Tax Bureau Louis L. Goldstein Treasury Bldg. P.O. Box 2999 Annapolis, MD 21404-0466 Phone: (410) 260-7314 Fax: (410) 974-3201 www.comp.state.md.us Montgomery County Department of Liquor Control 16650 Crabbs Branch Way Rockville, MD 20855 Phone: (240) 777-1900 Fax: (240) 777-1962 www.montgomerycountymd.gov Worcester County Liquor Control Board 5363 Snow Hill Road Snow Hill, MD 21863 Phone: (410) 632-1250 Fax: (410) 632-3010 www.liquormrt.com	Prohibited. Homebrewing is permitted on licensed facilities. This license will allow the holder to establish a facility where family wine and beer may be consumed. However, the holder of the permit may not engage in the production of homebrew, and may only provide the equipment, ingredients, and instructions. Samples may be distributed but are limited to 200-milliliters per sample.
Massachusetts Alcoholic Beverages Control Commission 239 Causeway Street Floor 1 Boston, MA 02114-2130 Phone: (617) 727-3040	Permitted. It is also permitted to store homebrew in a private residence.

Michigan* Liquor Control Commission P.O. Box 30005 Lansing, MI 48909 Phone: (517) 322-1345 www.michigan.gov/lara	Permitted. Must be brewed at home for personal consumption. The home-brewer is allowed to gift up to 20 gallons per calendar year to persons over 21 years of age for private consumption.
Minnesota Minnesota Department of Public Safety Liquor Control Division Alcohol and Gambling and Enforcement Division 444 Cedar St. Suite 133 St. Paul, MN 55101-5133 Phone: (651) 296-6979 TTY: (651) 282-6555	Permitted. The natural fermentation of beer is permitted without a license. The Minnesota statutes are not specific but private consumption is certainly allowed.
Mississippi* Alcoholic Beverage Control 1286 Gluckstadt Road Madison, MS 39110 Mailing Address: P. O. Box 540 Madison, MS 39130-0540 Phone: (601) 856-1301 www.dor.ms.gov	Prohibited. Wine is acceptable to produce for private consumption only. Beer and other forms of malt liquor and spirituous liquors are illegal to homebrew.
Missouri Division of Alcohol and Tobacco Control P.O. Box 837 Jefferson City, MO 65102 Phone: (573) 751-2333	Permitted. Nonintoxicating beer (less than 3.2% alcohol by weight) and intoxicating liquor may be manufactured. Limits are subject to federal law.
Montana* Montana Department of Revenue Citizens Services PO Box 5805 Helena, MT 59604-5805 Phone: 444-6900 Toll Free: (866) 859-2254 www.revenue.mt.gov	Permitted. Limits coincide with federal law.

Nebraska Nebraska Liquor Control Commission 301 Centennial Mall South P.O. Box 95046 Lincoln, NE 68509-5046 Phone: (402) 471-2571	Permitted. Homebrew must be fermented. The distillation process is prohibited.
Nevada Carson City 1550 E. College Parkway Suite 115 Carson City, NV 89706 Phone: (775) 687-4892 Reno 4600 Kietzke Lane Building O Room 263 Reno, NV 89502 Phone: (775) 688-1295 Elko 850 Elm Street #2 P.O. Box 1750 Elko, NV 89803 Phone: (775) 738-8461 Las Vegas Grant Sawyer Office Building 555 E. Washington Ave Suite 1300 Las Vegas, NV 89101 Phone: (702) 486-2300	Possibly Prohibited. The sale and distribution of alcohol is prohibited in Nevada without a special license. Homebrew does not fall under the statute and private consumption is not addressed. Each township is under specific jurisdiction.
New Hampshire* Headquarters and Warehousing 50 Storrs Street PO Box 503 Concord, NH 03301 Phone: (603) 230-7015 Bureau of Enforcement 57 Regional Drive Suite 8 Concord, NH 03301 www.nh.gov/liquor	Permitted. Homebrewers must be at least 21 years of age. Production limits coincide with federal law.

New Jersey New Jersey Department of Law and Public Safety Division of Alcoholic Beverage Control 140 East Front Street P.O. Box 087 Trenton, NJ 08625-0087 Phone: (609) 984-2830	Permitted. Requires an annual state permit. Homebrewers must be at least 21 years of age and produce no more than 200 gallons per calendar year.
New Mexico New Mexico Regulation & Licensing Department Alcohol and Gaming Division 725 St. Michael's Drive P.O. Box 25101 Santa Fe, NM 87504-5101 Phone: (505) 827-7066 New Mexico Department of Public Safety Special Investigations Division 6301 Indian School NE Suite 310 Albuquerque, NM 87110 Phone: (505) 841-8053	Possibly Permitted. New Mexico legislation attempts to regulate the sale of alcoholic beverages. As homebrewing is an aspect of private consumption, manufacture for personal use may be acceptable.
New York New York State Liquor Authority Division of Alcoholic Beverage Control Zone 1 State Liquor Authority 317 Lenox Ave. 4th Floor New York, NY 10027 Phone: (212) 961-8385	

Zone 2 State Liquor Authority 80 S. Swan St. Suite 900 Albany, NY 12210-8002 Phone: (518) 474-3114 Syracuse District State Liquor Authority 333 E. Washington St. Room 205 Syracuse, NY 13202 Phone: (315) 428-4198 Zone 3 State Liquor Authority 535 Washington St. Suite 303 Buffalo, NY 14203 Phone: (716) 847-3035	Permitted. Must be brewed for personal consumption only.
North Carolina* North Carolina Alco- holic Beverage Control Commission 400 East Tryon Rd Raleigh, NC 27610 Mailing Address: 4307 Mail Service Center Raleigh, NC 27699-4307 Phone: (919) 779-0700 www.abc.nc.gov	Permitted. No permits required for personal consumption of homebrew. Wine may also be homebrewed but must be manufactured with native products.
North Dakota North Dakota Office of the State Tax Commissioner Alcohol Tax Section 600 East Boulevard Avenue Bismarck, ND 58505-0599 Phone: (701) 328-2702	Permitted. Although there is no specific legislation pertaining to homebrew, North Dakota follows federal law.
Ohio* Division of Liquor Control 6606 Tussing Road Reynoldsburg, OH 43068 Phone: (614) 644-2411 www.com.ohio.gov/liqr	Possibly Prohibited. Homebrewing is not mentioned in the statute. A license is required for the sale and distribution of beer.

Oklahoma Alcoholic Beverage Law Enforcement Commission 4545 N. Lincoln Blvd. Suite 270 Oklahoma City, OK 73105 Phone: (405) 521-3484 The Oklahoma Tax Commission 2501 N. Lincoln Blvd. Oklahoma City, OK 73194-0004 Phone: (405) 521-4557	Permitted. With a permit obtained from the Alcoholic Beverage Laws Enforcement Commission, nonintoxicating beer is allowed to be homebrewed for personal use and activities. Homebrewed beer must be less than 3.2% alcohol by weight. Limited to 200 gallons per calendar year.
Oregon* Oregon Liquor Control Commission 9079 SE McLoughlin Blvd. Portland, OR 97222-7355 Mailing address: PO Box 22297 Milwaukie, OR 97269-2297 Phone: (503) 872-5000 Toll Free: (800) 452-6522 www.oregon.gov/OLCC	Permitted. Oregon has a vibrant homebrewing community. Oregon state laws coincide with federal regulations for homebrewing. SB444 recently made this possible.
Pennsylvania* Pennsylvania Liquor Control Board Commonwealth of Pennsylvania Northwest Office Building Harrisburg, PA 17124-0001 Phone: (717) 783-7637 TTY: (717) 772-3725 www.lcb.state.pa.us	Permitted. No license is required for homebrewers that produce no more than 200 gallons per calendar year and do not manufacture in order to sell. Homebrew may be used at organized affairs and recreational activities.

Rhode Island Liquor Enforcement and Compliance 233 Richmond Street Suite 200 Providence, RI 02903-4213 Phone: (401) 222-2562 Division of Commercial Licensing and Regulation 233 Richmond Street Suite 230 Providence, RI 02903 Phone: (401) 462-9506	Permitted. Homebrewers may manufac- ture for personal use.
South Carolina South Carolina Department of Revenue & Taxation Alcohol Beverage Licensing Section 301 Gervais St. P.O. Box 125 Columbia, SC 29214-0137 Phone: (803) 737-5000	Permitted. Nonintoxicating homebrew (less than 5% alcohol by weight) is per- mitted to be manufactured for personal use.
South Dakota South Dakota Department of Revenue & Regulation Division of Special Taxes 445 E. Capitol Avenue Pierre, SD 57501-3185 Phone: (605) 773-3311	Permitted. No license or permit required. Permitted for private con- sumption only. Limited to 200 gallons per calendar year.
Tennessee Tennessee Alcoholic Bever- age Commission 226 Capitol Blvd. Building Room 600 Nashville, TN 37219-0755 Phone: (615) 741-1602	Permitted. Subject to federal law. Trans- portation of homebrew must be limited to 5 gallons for recreational use.

Texas Texas Alcoholic Beverage Commission 5806 Mesa Dr. P.O. Box 13127 Capitol Station Austin, TX 78711-3127 Phone: (512) 206-3333	Permitted. Homebrewers are limited to 200 gallons per calendar year. Consumption at events and activities is also permitted with permission from the commission for the delivery of homebrew. Distilling is prohibited.
Utah* Department of Alcoholic Beverage Control 1625 South 900 West Salt Lake City, UT 84104 Phone: (801) 977-6800 Fax: (801) 977-6888 www.abc.utah.gov	Permitted. Utah limits coincide with federal law limits. Transportation of homebrew must be less than 1 liter per person over 21 years of age, or less than 1 liter per category in a taste test/competition.
Vermont* Department of Liquor Control 13 Green Mountain Drive Montpelier, VT 05620-4501 Phone: (802) 828-2345 www.state.vt.us/dlc	Permitted. The manufacture of homebrew is permitted as long as the quantity produced is under federal limits. The transportation of homebrew for recreational activities is acceptable; however the event's sponsor must provide written notice to the ABC agency at least 10 days prior to any festivities.
Virginia* VA ABC's main office: 2901 Hermitage Road Richmond, VA 23220 Mailing address: Virginia Dept. of Alcoholic Beverage Control P. O. Box 27491 Richmond, VA 23261 Phone: (804) 213-4413 www.abc.state.va.us	Permitted. Homebrewing is permitted in the home as well as in specialty brewing shops for personal consumption. Limits are subject to federal law.

Washington*
Washington Business License
Services
Department of Licensing
P.O. Box 9034
Olympia, WA 98504-3075
Phone: (360) 586-2784
www.dol.wa.gov/business/
licensing

Washington State Liquor
Control Board
3000 Pacific Avenue
P.O. Box 3098
Olympia, WA 98504-3098
Phone: (360) 664-1600
www.liq.wa.gov

Permitted. For personal use only. Transportation of up to 20 gallons for recreational activities is acceptable permitting the homebrew is not for sale.

West Virginia*
West Virginia Alcohol Beverage Control Commission
Enforcement & Licensing
Division
322 70th St. S.E.
Charleston, WV 25304-2900
Phone: (304) 558-2481
Toll Free: (800) 642-8208
www.abca.wv.gov

Possibly Prohibited. Virginia legislation makes an exception for homebrewed wine but not for beer. It is illegal to manufacture and sell alcoholic liquor without the correct license. However, nonintoxicating (less than 6% by volume) beer is not included in West Virginia's definition of alcoholic liquor.

Wisconsin
Wisconsin Alcohol &
Tobacco Enforcement
Department of Revenue
2135 Rimrock Road
Madison, WI 53713
Phone: (608) 266-2776

Permitted. Homebrewing is permitted to be consumed in the home by the brewer, family and friends. Not to be sold, or taken off-premises.

Wyoming*
Wyoming Liquor
Commission
1520 East 5th Street
Cheyenne, WY 82002
Phone: (307) 777-7231
www.revenue.state.wy.us

Permitted. Homebrewing is permitted in limited quantities for the brewer's consumption only. Wyoming follows federal law. A license is required from the Wyoming ABC agency in order to sell.

RESOURCES

Periodicals

Fuller, Tom, "Keep Your Brewhouse in Peak Form," *Brew Your Own*, December 1996.

Conn, Denny, "Cheap and Easy Batch Sparging," *Brew Your Own*, January/February 2004.

Colby, C. & Spencer J., "Lautering Method Showdown," *Brew Your Own*, May/June 2011, pg 50–51.

Fodor, Alex, "Feel the Mash Heat," *Brew Your Own*, January/February 2004.

Colby, C. & Spencer J., "The Effects of Storage Conditions on Homebrew Quality," *Brew Your Own*, March/April 2011, pg 32–36.

Coghe, S., Gheeraert, B. Michiels, A. Delvaux, F. "Development of Maillard Reaction Realted Characteristics During Malt Roasting," *J. Inst. Brew*, 112(2) 148–156 (2006).

Van Opstaele, F. DeRouck, G. De Clippeleer, J., Aerts, G., DeCooman, L, "Analytical and Sensory Assessment of Hoppy Aroma and Bitterness of Conventionally Hopped and Advanced Hopped Pilsner Beers," *J. Inst. Brew*, 116(4) 445–448 (2010).

Erten, H., Tanguler, H., Cakiroz, H., "The Effect of Pitching Rate on Fermentation and Flavor Compounds in High Gravity Brewing," *J. Inst. Brew*, 113(1), 75–79 (2007).

Strong, Gordon, "Mastering Malt: Selecting the Best Base for your Beer," *Zymurgy*, Vol. 34, No.3, 18-23 (2011).

Books

Priest, F.G. & Stewart, Graham, *Handbook of Brewing*, CRC Press/Thomson Publishing, 2006.

Palmer, John, *How to Brew*, Brewers Publications, Boulder, Colorado, 2006.

Daniels, Ray, *Designing Great Beers*, Brewers Publications, Boulder, Colorado, 2000.

Papazian, Charlie, *The New Complete Joy of Homebrewing, Third Edition*, Harper Paperbacks, 2003.

Papazian, Charlie, *The Homebrewer's Companion*, Harper Paperbacks, 2003.

Papazian, Charlie, *Zymurgy for the Homebrewer and Beer Lover*, William Morrow Cookbooks, 1998.

Smith, Greg, *Beer In America*, Brewers Publications, Boulder, Colorado, 1998.

White, Christ & Zainasheff, Jamil, *Yeast: The Practical Guide to Beer Fermentation*, Brewers Publications, Boulder, Colorado, 2010

Jackson, Michael, *Michael Jackson's Beer Companion*, Second Edition, Running Press, 1997.

Foster, Terry, *Porter*, Brewers Publications, 1992.

GLOSSARY

A

Acetaldehyde—Acetaldehyde is formed during fermentation as a precursor to alcohol and presents as a cider-like off-flavor.

Acetic Acid—An off flavor resembling vinegar.

Acidity—Can refer either to the acidic character of the beer or a direct measurement of the pH of the wort during the mash.

Adjunct—Supplementary grains that are added to the main mash ingredients in a brew. Adjuncts, when mashed with malted grains will result in a conversion to sugars.

Aeration—The process in which air is dissolved into or circulated through a liquid. When brewing beer, the wort must be thoroughly aerated before pitching yeast in order to promote healthy yeast growth and reproduction.

Airlock—A device used to simultaneously allow the escape of **carbon dioxide** and prevent exposure of the beer to air during the fermentation process, thus avoiding oxidation.

Alcohol—A class of compounds composed of carbon, oxygen, and hydrogen. Ethanol (C_2H_5OH) is one of those compounds and is the primary alcohol produced when brewing beer.

Alcohol Content—The percentage of alcohol in a specific beverage. It can be measured by volume or by weight.

Alpha Acid—Present in the resin glands of the cones of the hop plant, alpha acids impart a bitter flavor to the beer. When boiling in the wort, alpha acids become isomerized, allowing them to dissolve into the wort. Commercial hops can be sold by the percentage by weight of alpha acids (% AA). A higher percentage and a long boil increases the potential bitterness.

Alpha Acid Units—See HBU.

Alpha Amylase—An enzyme that is responsible for breaking down the starches found in grains into fermentable sugars by cleaving the starch chain in the middle. This enzyme is most efficient in the higher ranges of mashing temperatures and tends to produce wort that has greater body.

Anaerobic Fermentation—Fermentation without exposure to oxygen. It is the primary process for fermentation used in brewing beer wherein yeast turns sugar to alcohol and carbon dioxide.

Aroma—In brewing, the aroma contributes to the perception of taste and the overall sensory experience as the tongue can only sense five distinct flavors: sweet, sour, bitter, salty, and savory.

Aroma Hops—Aroma Hops are added late in the brewing process, contributing aroma but very little bitterness.

Attenuation—A measure of the drop in the specific gravity in the beer as it ferments. In other words, it is the ability of yeast to ferment sugars within the wort. Yeast strains will often have an average attenuation rate, which allows control over the final flavors and body of each brew.

B

Barley—A hardy cereal grain, it serves as a key ingredient and base malt in the brewing process. Both six- and two-row barley are commonly used.

Barrel—A wooden vessel traditionally used to standardize the measurement of capacity for a specific commodity. Today, a barrel is equivalent to 31 U.S. gallons and is the main unit for commercial beer production. A "keg" is half a barrel.

Beta Amylase—An enzyme that is responsible for breaking down the starches found in grains into fermentable sugars. Unlike alpha amylase, beta amylase is most efficient in the lower ranges of mashing temperatures and cleaves the starch chains at the ends.

Bittering Hops—Hops added at the beginning of a boil in order to attain higher levels of bitterness. The higher the alpha acid concentration in the hops, the more bitter the beer will be.

Blow-Off Tube—A large-diameter tube utilized to allow carbon dioxide and krausen to escape during fermentation. When rigged correctly, a blow-off tube can serve as an effective airlock.

Body—The substantial character of a beer, it is the complexity and fullness that results from residual malt sugars in the beer.

Break—Break is produced when the proteins in the wort coagulate, resulting in a clearer beer.

C

Carbon Dioxide (CO_2) A colorless, odorless gas resulting from fermentation. Although most escapes through the airlock during the fermentation process, the residual carbon dioxide produces the effervescent, or bubbly, quality in beer.

Carbonation—The process of impregnating the beer with dissolved carbon dioxide gas. It can also refer to the amount of CO_2 in a beer. Carbonation occurs naturally during fermentation, but can also be forced by placing the contents of a beverage under pressure.

Carboy—A large, wide container with a short, narrow neck. Usually made of glass or plastic, a carboy can be used in primary fermentation. A secondary carboy is sometimes used when transferring beer after the fermentation process has ended. In brewing, a carboy is also known as a demijohn.

Clarify—To make the beer more clear or brilliant. There are many processes which can clarify a beer, all of which remove suspended or insoluble particles.

Cold Break—When wort is chilled quickly causing proteins to coagulate, the result of which is break.

Concentrate—Concentrated wort is available to brewers in the form of malt extract. By condensing wort through boiling or vacuum evaporation, transportation and production become cheaper and easier.

Conditioning—Occurs after primary fermentation. It involves three processes: maturation, clarification, and stabilization. Carbonation also occurs during conditioning.

Conversion—The process of changing from one form or state into another (e.g., the chemical change from starch into sugar).

D

Decant—To pour gently on an incline in order to separate mixtures. Decanting a beer will prevent the disturbing of sediment.

Decoction—A method of extraction by boiling. Decoction was used universally before temperatures could be accurately measured and maintained. During decoction, a portion of the mash is removed and brought to a boil. When it is returned to the main mash, the temperature raises creating caramelized sugars and gelatinized starches, providing flavors which might otherwise be difficult to attain.

Demijohn—*See* Carboy.

Dextrin—A long chain carbohydrate that is not susceptible to fermentation. Residual dextrins affect the body of the beer.

Diacetyl ($C_4H_6O_2$)—A natural by-product of fermentation, this aromatic compound is responsible for buttery or butterscotch flavors and scents in beer. While the presence of diacetyl in large

amounts is generally considered a flaw, low levels are characteristic of certain types of beers .

Distillation—The process of heating a substance into a vapor and
subsequently condensing it by means of refrigeration back into
liquid form. The resulting solution is much more concentrated
than the original. Distillation is the process by which hard liq-
uors (such as gin or whiskey) are made.

DME (Dried or Dry Malt Extract)—Used exclusively as a substitute
for base malt in homebrewing, DME is the concentrated form of
base malt. *See* Concentrate and Malt Extract.

DMS (Dimethyl Sulfide)—DMS presents itself as an off-flavor
resembling cooked corn or vegetable matter. It is developed
when the wort is heated, although it is generally evaporated out
during the boil.

Draff—The grain refuse that remains in the lauter tun after sparging.
Also known as lees or dregs.

Dry Hopping—The process of adding hops for aromatic effect during
or after fermentation.

E

Enzymes—Complex proteins that have the capability to catalyze bio-
chemical reactions by either forming or breaking bonds. During
the fermentation process, enzymes break down starches to produce sugar which is in turn used by the yeast to produce alcohol.

Ethyl Alcohol—*See* Ethanol.

Ethanol (C2H5OH)—Produced during the brewing process. *See*
Alcohol.

Extraction Efficiency—A measure of the sugars produced during the
homebrew process compared with a theoretical maximum for the
specific grains used. A typical range would fall between 60 and
80 percent.

F

False Bottom—A perforated object in the bottom of the lauter tun to allow for the drainage of sweet wort, or the liquid runoff of the grains. These are available in a variety of materials and can also be homemade.

Fermentation—The process by which yeast turns sugars into energy, alcohol, carbon dioxide, more yeast, and other by-products.

Fermentation Lock—*See* Airlock.

Filtration—The process of removing yeast and other large particles from the brew. In essence, the separation of solids from liquids.

Final Gravity—The measurement of specific gravity after the fermentation process is completed.

Finings—Usually added at the end of the homebrewing process in order to filter and clarify a brew. There are various materials in common use which cause solids and suspended particles to precipitate, making the filtration process easier. Finings are usually removed unless they form an acceptable and stable sediment.

Flocculation—The tendency of yeast to clump together and fall out of suspension.

G

Gelatinization—The process by which heat and water break down the bonds in starch molecules resulting in the even disbursement of the starches throughout the water. Full gelatinization occurs around 149 degrees Fahrenheit. Gelatinization directly affects extraction efficiency.

Grain—Seeds and grasses that are cultivated for their edibility. It is the seeds that are used in malting and brewing. Also referred to as cereals.

Grain Bill—The grains used in any given homebrew recipe. Also known as mash bill.

Grant—Although most homebrewers do not use grants, it is a small copper or iron vessel that serves as a buffer between the lauter **tun** and a pump. During a **sparge**, the **wort** is run through the grant creating easy access for the brewer for monitoring.

Gravity—*See* SG (Specific Gravity).

Grist—Grains and adjuncts that have been separated from their chaff in preparation for grinding or brewing. The grist serves as the raw material for a mash before water is added.

H

HBU (Homebrew Bitterness Units)—Calculated by multiplying the percentage of alpha acids by the weight in ounces of the hops. Also known as alpha acid units, this measure is the potential bitterness level of any given brew.

HLT (Hot Liquor Tank)—The storage vessel for hot water to be used in sparging.

Hop Back—A vessel used at the end of the boiling process that allows hot wort to be run through a bed of hops. The hops act as a filter removing break material, while imparting flavor and aroma.

Hops—The ripened cones of the female flower clusters of the hop plant, hops are brewed into beer with the intention of balancing the sweetness of malt with bitterness. This bitterness derives from the resin gland in the female plant. Hops are prized for their flavorful and aromatic qualities and are an integral ingredient in brewing.

Hot Liquor—The hot water used for sparging.

Hot-Side Aeration—The introduction of oxygen into the wort, causing oxidation and potentially damaging a brew.

Humulone $C_{21}H_{30}O_5$—A type of alpha acid, it is an orange or yellow resin in hops that lend the beer its bitter qualities. Humulone also acts as an antibiotic.

Hydrometer—A glass instrument used to measure the specific gravity of wort by calculating the ratio of density to the density of water. Hydrometers come equipped with different scales and are useful in monitoring the fermentation process and calculating the alcohol content.

I

IBU (International Bittering Units)—While HBU is the scale for potential bitterness, IBU is the scale used to accurately measure the degree of bitterness in any given beer. While this is usually done commercially, there are ways for homebrewers to estimate the measure.

Iso-Alpha Acid—An alpha acid after it has been isomerized. Isomerization occurs in beer when the hops in the wort are boiled for extended periods of time. The longer the boil, the more iso-alpha acids will be produced.

Isomerize—When a compound is isomerized, the chemical composition is rearranged although it remains the same compound.

K

Krausen—Usually defined as the foamy head that forms on top of the brew during the initial fermentation phases, but "to krausen" is also the process of carbonating beer by adding wort to the fermented or finished product.

L

Lautering—*See* Sparging.

Lauter Tun—The vessel in which sugars are extracted from the grain. Lauter tuns come in a variety of available and homemade materials; it is often combined with the mash tun. Sparging, or lautering, takes place within the lauter tun.

Liquor—Water, or strike water, which is mixed in with the grist. *See* Hot Liquor.

LME (Liquid Malt Extract)—Malt extract in liquid form. *See* Concentrate and Malt Extract.

Lovibond—A measure of the color of any given beer.

M

Malt—Grains which have been germinated and dried to produce the enzymes that are needed to begin the fermentation process.

Malt Extract—A sweet concentrated form of wort that is commonly used amongst homebrewers. *See* Concentrate.

Maltodextrin—An unfermentable carbohydrate derived from the partial hydrolysis of starches. It can be used as an additive to add body and head retention.

Mash—The process of converting starches to sugars, by steeping the crushed grains in order to allow enzymes to break the long-chain starches into short-chain sugars.

Mash In—The initial stages of mashing wherein the liquor and grain bill are first mixed.

Mash Out—After the enzyme rest, the temperature of the mash is raised again, fixing the composition of the wort. If the lauter tun is separate from the mash tun, the contents are transferred at this stage. This step is not always performed.

Mash Tun—A vessel wherein liquor and malt are mixed. In commercial brewing facilities, there are usually separate vessels for mashing and lautering. Homebrewers often use a combined vessel referred to as an MLT.

MLT (Mash/Lauter Tun)—A combination of a mash tun and a lauter tun.

Modified—Meaning a modified starch. The degree of change in composition of the starch is what is known as modified. The most commonly used malts are fully modified.

N

Noble Hops—Traditionally refers to four varieties from central Europe which are low in bitterness and high in aroma. Many other hop varieties are variations on these four.

O

OG (Original Gravity)—The measure of specific gravity of wort before the fermentation process begins.

Oxidation—Occurs when (1.) a hydrogen molecule is lost in a compound (2.) a compound gains an oxygen molecule or (3.) when electrons are wholly or partially removed from a molecule. The result often leads to stale and unpleasant flavors in beer. Oxidation is why carboys and airlocks are necessary components of the homebrew process.

Oxygen (O)—Although oxygen is necessary at the start of the fermentation process, oxygen exposure should be otherwise avoided to reduce the chances of spoiling a brew. *See* Oxidation.

P

pH—A measure of acidity or alkalinity of a given solution. This measure is important specifically in homebrewing as it directly affects the efficiency of the enzymes during the mashing period.

Phytase—A class of enzymes that are responsible for the breakdown of phytic acid into myo-inositol and phosphoric acid.

Phytic Acid—Found in the seeds of grains and also in yeast. The conversion of phytic acid will lower the pH of a brew, raising the acidity levels.

Pitch—A term used for the adding of dry or liquid yeast to cooled and aerated wort.

Primary Fermentation—Occurs after pitching. It is most notably known for its visual activity with the formation of krausen. *See* Fermentation.

Priming—Adding sugars to the fermented product before bottling which results in the carbonation process.

Protease—An enzyme that restricts the gelatinization of proteins, resulting in better wort filtration and higher extract efficiency.

R

Refractometer—An instrument that measures the sucrose content of a beer through a refraction index. Refractometers are available with a variety of scales and functions.

Rest—Holding at specific temperatures while mashing to activate enzymes in order to begin specific conversion processes. Examples include protein rests, saccharification rests, and acid rests.

S

Saccharometer—A type of hydrometer that measures the sugar in fermentable wort by means of specific gravity.

Sanitizer—A disinfectant product that kills microbacteria, which have the potential to contaminate tools, instruments, and the beer. Equipment should be sanitized before each use.

Secondary Fermentation—After primary fermentation, the beer may or may not be transferred to a secondary fermentation container. During secondary fermentation, beer is further clarified and aged. *See* Fermentation.

SG (Specific Gravity)—A measure taken with a hydrometer. It is the ratio of the density of water to the density of a brew. As fermentation begins, the SG decreases.

Sparge—A process done in the lauter tun, it is the addition of water to the mash as the wort drains. This process washes the sugars from the grains as the water passes through.

Starch—Produced by plants as an energy store, starches are broken down during malting and mashing to produce sugars in the wort, which are further modified into alcohol during fermentation.

Starter—Used initially to aid the fermentation process. A brewer's starter might consist of wort and yeast in order to produce higher yeast populations for more efficient fermentation.

Strike Temperature—The temperature of the strike water or liquor.

Strike Water—*See* Hot Liquor.

Stuck Fermentation—Occurs when the fermentation process ends prematurely due to dormant yeast. Stuck fermentation may occur because of yeast deficiency, improper yeast nutrition, incorrect temperatures, or other causes.

Siphoning—The act of transferring beer from one container to the next through a siphon. The siphon is an inverted U-shaped tube that uses gravity to pull the liquid up and through. This is also sometimes referred to as racking.

T

Tannin—A vegetable substance found in the husks of grains which produce astringent bitter flavors.

Terminal Gravity—*See* Final Gravity.

Trub—Dead flocculated yeast, break material, and other debris that collects in the bottom of the beer during and after fermentation.

V

Vinegar—Can be made from unhopped beer and can be known as malt vinegar. Vinegar is produced from the fermentation of ethanol.

Vorlauf—The process of running wort out of the mash or lauter tun and into the grant or back into the mash tub to be recirculated through the grain bed, the result of which is a more clarified brew.

W

Water Lock—*See* Airlock.

Wild Yeast—A yeast strain that was not intentionally introduced to a specific batch of beer. Most of these strains are ruinous but a small percentage can be utilized.

Wine Thief—A glass or plastic pipette used to extract a small amount of beer from a fermentation device for testing.

Wort—The liquid extracted from the mashing process before the yeast is added and fermentation begins. In essence, wort is unfermented beer.

Y

Yeast—A type of fungi used to convert carbohydrates and sugars into alcohol. Brewing yeast strains differ from baking yeast strains and are typically chosen for specific functions such as the ability to flocculate, their tolerance to alcohol, and by-product production.

Yeast Nutrient Additives that promote and increase healthy yeast growth to ensure vigorous fermentation. These additives, such as certain minerals, serve as a food source for yeast strains.

Z

Zymurgy—The science and art of alcoholic beverage fermentation.

ACKNOWLEDGMENTS

THIS BOOK WOULD not have been possible without the help of many people, including Greg DiRubbio, who has been brewing with me since Day One, and Ryan Crook, who was instrumental in creating the opportunity to write this. A special thanks is in order to the good folks at Brooklyn Homebrew, who allowed me to invade their space in order to take pictures, and the same goes to Rodrigo and Melissa at GoodBrewing.com, who provided most of the base ingredients used in the photos. Phil Shaw, Ryan Kahler, and John Cope provided photographs, as did Weyermann Specialty Malts and Muntons Malted Ingredients Inc. Finally, none of this would have been possible without my editor Joseph Sverchek, our research assistant Jamie Sanford, and the other staff at Skyhorse Publishing.

et occabo. Cum qui unt ea di te perferia samet veliscides quia nobitiusam exerupti quias ut hari re volupturibus magnihit verum velessit ut eaquaeseque volum ullis elestiame dolupti isciis aut reptatur sitatas mi, con consenem necto bea non reped quaspictio quid quo velicias

INDEX